Exavier

MW00960815

CHERI FIELDS

The End

Bible Prophecy Study for Teens

First published by Spiral Shell Communications 2021

Copyright © 2021 by Cheri Fields

All rights reserved. No part of this publication may be reproduced, stored or transmitted in any form or by any means, electronic, mechanical, photocopying, recording, scanning, or otherwise without written permission from the publisher. It is illegal to copy this book, post it to a website, or distribute it by any other means without permission.

This book is designed to work with any and all translations of the Bible. Every attempt has been made to accomodate the differences between them, but the author is most familiar with the King James Version and thinks it's beautiful, so that's the one used for quotations.

First edition

This book was professionally typeset on Reedsy. Find out more at reedsy.com

Contents

Studying the Future

Blessed is he that readeth, and they that hear the words of this prophecy, and keep those things which are written therein: for the time is at hand. Revelation 1:3 KJV

The Wrong View of Prophecy Has Destroyed Many People

Did you know the Jews rejected Jesus in part because they hadn't studied their prophets carefully enough? Daniel had told them exactly when to expect the Messiah, and they missed him. Even if they had been reading carefully what the Messiah was going to be like they would have figured it out. Instead, they focused on what they wanted to see: a Law-and-Traditions superhero who would squash the Romans.

Ever since then, Jews, who above all loved the teachings of their forefathers, have explained away and hidden many of the prophecies about the Messiah. Most Jews barely know Isaiah 53 is in their Scriptures—because its prophecy fits far too well with what happened to Jesus.

I won't get into all the mess modern people have made of their view of life, other people, and their faith because of opinionated ideas about the End Times. You will probably learn more about this as you get older, but there have been things like forbidding people to marry or even date certain people, careless spending of money, new Christians not being taught how to handle persecution, and rejecting godly ministers just because they don't see The End exactly the same way. The list of dangers goes on and on—and that's before we get to what false Christian cults do with prophecy!

So, if you don't want to fall for any of these traps, understanding what God does—and does not—teach us about how he takes over the world is inescapable. And, if you don't let it scare you too much, it's fun!

The Far End of History

Have you ever wondered what the world is going to be like in the future? What will my own life be like? What will happen to my country in a hundred years?

For thousands of years, people have asked these questions and come up with ideas about how history will end. Some worldviews imagine that time goes round and round in circles, never really going anywhere new. The secular scientists of today recognize that we cannot create new energy; their worldview pictures that, at some point, the entire universe is going to run out of usable heat and light and everything will go dark in something called "heat death."

Not too exciting to picture, is it?

As human beings we are stuck in time; we can study the past and observe the present, but we can only guess about the future. But God is already there, and he has told us enough about what he has planned for the world, and each of us, to give us a deep and unshakable hope!

Layers of Prophecy

For centuries people have wondered why some biblical prophecies were so clearly fulfilled at some point in history while other bits don't fit what has already happened. Let me show you some clear examples of a split prophecy like this:

Ezekiel was one of the Jewish captives Nebuchadnezzar dragged off to Babylon. Later we'll be looking at the end of his book where he has a lot to say about the end of history, but right now I'd like you to check out something he prophesied that fully happened long ago. In **chapter 26** he gives a prediction about the city of Tyre, the capital of the Phoenicians who invented our alphabet and who were the top sea-faring people in ancient times.

In **verses 4–5**, Ezekiel describes how the city will be so thoroughly destroyed fishermen will spread their nets out on its bedrock that has been scraped bare. Then, in **verses 7–13** it announces Nebuchadnezzar himself will besiege and enter the city before announcing again in **verse 14** that it will be turned into bare rock. Then, three chapters later in **Ezekiel 29:18–20** God says he's going to reward Nebuchadnezzar with the wealth of Egypt since he didn't get paid for all his work destroying Tyre.

What is going on? Did God give Ezekiel a false prophecy? Hardly.

Here's how it played out in history: the Babylonians under Nebuchadnezzar did indeed lay siege to Tyre and enter it, but only after 13 years of struggle when the Phoenicians with their wealth had escaped to a small island half a mile off the coast. It wasn't until hundreds of years later that Alexander the Great had his men throw the rubble of the abandoned city into the sea that the rock was scraped bare and the city plundered.

God's prophecy did come true, but some of the verses took hundreds of years longer than others to be fulfilled.

Jesus himself used this splitting of prophecy. Soon after Jesus started his public ministry he traveled back to his hometown of Nazareth, no longer as a handworker, but now as a preacher. Let's read about it in **Luke 4:16–21**. On the Sabbath they invited Jesus to give the sermon and, like a good pastor today, he started with a Bible passage. Then he sits down to explain the verses.

But wait! Keep your hand in Luke and find **Isaiah 61:1–2**. You can see exactly what Jesus was reading, although a few words are probably different because Luke was using the Greek version of Isaiah. Now, look at where Jesus stopped—he put away the Bible *right in the middle of a sentence.*

Why would he do that? Because the "day of vengeance of our God" is one of the biggest pieces of End Time prophecy. And it wasn't time for that 'day' yet. Jesus hadn't come that time to avenge himself on his enemies, he had come to suffer and die. But it *was* time for the first part of Isaiah's prediction. And, guess what, we are still waiting 2,000 years later for the phrase Jesus didn't finish reading.

Then, during Peter's first sermon with the help of the Holy Spirit, he quotes a prophecy. In **Acts 2:16–21**, he recites **Joel 2:28–32**. Anyone who had been

3

in Jerusalem when Jesus was killed had seen the darkness, although the rest of the "blood, fire, and pillars of smoke" seems kind of odd. But remember, chapter breaks in the Bible were not there in Peter's day, they came a thousand years later.

Look at what Joel says at the beginning of **chapter 3**. He predicts all nations will be gathered to the valley of Jehoshaphat, and God will avenge the evil they have done to his people.

That has still not happened 2,000 years later.

Finally, let's read the only writer in the Bible that calls Satan's main human tool the "Antichrist." Of all places, this title is found most clearly in **1 John 2**. Let's read **verses 18-22**. The first time we see him here it's easy to see why so many recognize this is the big bad guy himself. He's been predicted to come and verse 22 says this man and his type deny both the Father and Jesus himself.

But what John says about there already being many antichrists tells us an important KEY about prophecy. There's the real thing, and it is absolutely sure, but there are usually more than one (in this case "many") copies from the same mold. Even John telling us we know it's the "end time" fits in this pattern. We'll soon see how all of time since Jesus rose into heaven has been part of the last times.

How do you wrap your mind around something that feels so out of focus like this? Some people picture it as the prophet is looking out across a landscape and seeing mountain peaks. Some bits are near, some predictions are on distant high peaks with the huge final events that wrap up history.

I like to think of it as a picture with several layers of clear paper on top. If you lift one sheet you can see which parts are now history, but others must still be in the future. And many pieces are drawn on all the layers, with history repeating itself to form the same basic picture.

Many people call these copycat events and characters "types." Two of the biggest examples of this are Elijah (both John the Baptist at Jesus's first coming and the Old Testament prophet returning before Jesus's second coming) and the Antichrist. This ultimate bad guy has shown up in characters from Genesis (Nimrod), the Prophets (Antiochus Epiphanes), to modern times

(Hitler), and the 'real' one is still in the future. These aren't the same human beings, but they follow the same worldview and methods. And why not?

After all, the main players—God and his demonic enemies—are the same today as they were in the Garden of Eden.

And I'll let you in on a big secret. God is the Creator and he is creative. When Satan broke away from God he lost his ability to invent anything new; 2 Corinthians 2:11 assumes we can know all his tricks, and he used exactly the same set of temptations (1 John 2:16) on Jesus in the desert (Matthew 4:3–10) that he pulled on Eve in the garden (Genesis 3:1–6). Every idea he has and every evil deed he convinces his people to do is a twisted version of what God does. And nothing he wants is any different than it was thousands of years ago.

This means any bad guy is going to be the same kind of character as all the other bad guys throughout history. The differences only happen because of what makes that person himself. People still bear a unique bit of God's image even when they go rotten.

The Bible is like a Jigsaw Puzzle, Detective's Case, and DNA

Have you ever put together a puzzle that had been done before? Sometimes whoever put it away will have left a few pieces connected together—it's like a hint speeding up the process of reassembling the picture.

With important concepts God has usually done this for us, and it's a good thing he did, because we do NOT get a picture of the finished puzzle on the outside of the box! While there are spots where key ideas get explained clearly enough we know they go together, there are a lot of smaller pieces we still have to find scattered all through the Bible.

What about detectives? They build up a picture of an event in the past by finding evidence and clues. Some clues are small and only make sense when more information is added, but some findings are so clear they become star witnesses that unlock the significance of the smaller pieces.

Also, one of the hallmarks of true eyewitness testimony is when different people report different versions of the same event. If each person's account lines up too neatly, the investigators start to wonder if they got together and made the whole thing up. God understands this concept, and, whether it is how the Gospels report on Jesus's life or how prophets report on the end of history, we see complementary but different versions across the Bible.

Then, one of my favorite discoveries: DNA. Scientists are having their minds blown as they literally unravel the mystery of the code that tells our cells what to do. It uses only 4 letters and always forms 3 letter words, but can give directions to make every protein and hormone in our body. Here's the low down:

DNA can be read forwards, backwards, and folded to bring distant sections together, each giving the cell a different message.

You've heard of palindromes like "Madam I'm Adam" where the letters can be read from right to left and be the same? With DNA the message is *different* backwards, but still real. And, what if you could fold them in and read "Ma, I am" too? That's what DNA does all the time!

Jesus is the inventor of DNA, and he is the one who created the Bible. Why would he be fancier with a cell than with his eternal Word?

—Oh, and most ancient Hebrew words were also formed with three letters. Doesn't that just blow your mind?

So, when you are reading the Bible to learn what God has to tell us about a subject, you will usually have a handful of starting-point passages that help guide your search. Then, once you've gotten these main ideas, you get to wander all over, looking for similar pieces that fit into the picture.

Two or Three (or dozens of) "Witnesses"

These were more noble than those in Thessalonica, in that they received the word with all readiness of mind, and searched the scriptures daily, whether those things were so. Acts 17:11

Anything new we learn isn't going to contradict the plain reading of something we already know. In fact, a KEY principle of Bible study is to remember what

God told judges to keep in mind when considering whether someone is telling the truth:

Read what God says in **Deuteronomy 19:15**. How many people have to say the same thing before a judge is to make his decision? God follows his own rule and tells us this is his unchanging standard in Deuteronomy 17:6; Numbers 35:30; Matthew 18:16; 2 Corinthians 13:1; 1 Timothy 5:19 and several more places.

So, if someone shares an idea they say comes from a verse in the Bible, check it out. The first place to start is with the verse's context. Was this really what the author meant? Does the idea fit with the ideas before and after it?

Even if the idea seems reasonable from the passage, if you cannot find the same idea anywhere else, especially if the idea clashes with other verses, do not believe the idea. God's word is true, he cannot and will not say one thing in one verse and say something that contradicts himself anywhere else. While there are a number of places the skeptics claim God has contradicted himself, when we are willing to submit our thinking to him, he helps us unravel the truth—and that is never contradictory.

We can use this format of using cornerstone passages and adding in other verses to study any topic you can imagine in the Bible, but this study is going to help us experience how this works using one of the most fascinating topics, the future of the universe!

Prophecy Uses lots of Colorful 'Characters'

We are going to meet a lot of people in this study, but not all of them will be human beings or even demons. Take a minute to look at **Proverbs 9**. The first part of the chapter walks us through a house being built, a party being prepared, and a marketing campaign being run—all by the lady "Wisdom." Then her rival, "Foolishness," makes her pitch for newbies to listen to her instead.

Scholars don't think there was a real human or angel named Wisdom. "She" is a symbol of an idea, a way of looking at the world. We're going to see lots of characters like this in prophecy.

Since Christianity was new there have been people who think *all* the characters in prophecy are like Lady Wisdom. On the other hand, many of us see the symbols represent real people, countries, and groups. But not all symbolic characters will be visible, so it takes discernment and thinking to tell which is which. We'll walk through these as they come up, just be ready for some bizarre-looking characters!

Keep Track of your Clues

Or, you might want to mark up your Bible and get a notebook.

I would have never dreamed of messing up my Bible as a girl. My mom had taught me never to scribble in a book; no way was I going to do that to God's own Word! But when I grew up, I ran into a lady who taught Bible studies and she *loved* marking all over her Bible. She used special pens and had a whole series of shapes she would draw to keep track of important ideas and things.

So, I decided to try it. My Bible isn't big enough to put pictures all through the words, plus I figured that would make it hard to read anyway, but I decided to use colored pencils and some special highlighters I found designed for the thin paper of our Bibles. As I started reading and marking this way I found it helped me notice all kinds of things I hadn't before. And it helps pass the time when the sermon is a little dull (don't tell my pastor!).

Oh, yes, be sure to write any notes in pencil. I've come back to a passage and realized some things I'd written down the last time were dead wrong. I even found out the hard way that colored pencils are great to use because they rub off if I decide to switch colors. If you study long enough, I guarantee this will happen to you too.

You don't have to mark your Bible for this study, and I suggest you talk with your parents about it first, but many people have found colors and notes in their Bibles help them understand and remember things better. It is also a great way to keep track of linked clues without having to remember all the references.

We're about to start a massive and wide-ranging study, so here are a couple of things you'll want to write down for yourself.

While the main passages are easy enough to keep straight, there are a number of smaller sections that help us understand the bigger ones. Any reference I've highlighted in bold is directly part of the study. You are responsible to look them up. A few additional references are there to support a claim I'm making, you can look them up for yourself, but you don't have to.

Many of these verses make great cross references. If you have room in the margins of your Bible, you can write them in there (I pulled this study together in part by going back to the collection in my Bible.)

Then, there are a bunch of "KEY"s to keep straight. It might be a good idea for you to collect these key ideas with their references in your notebook to really grab hold of the concept. Remember, many of these are things seminary professors, pastors, and authors have trouble with. But the Bible is as much for you as it is for them—grab its truth!

Jesus is our Key Witness

Considering Jesus is the Word of God himself (John 1:1), it makes sense to start with what he has to say about the future. And, while we'll be getting to *the Book of the Revelation of Jesus Christ* eventually, we're going to start much earlier in the New Testament.

Let's set things up.

Jesus is hours away from his death. He's spending the last few days of his life in Jerusalem, giving his people a last chance to turn away from their attempts to earn God's favor by being good. He's just finished saying such horrible things to the Pharisees (read Matthew 23 to see how ruthless Jesus was) they cannot wait for a chance to kill him while the common people aren't around to stop them.

But Jesus's disciples don't understand what's happening. They have always pictured the coming of the Messiah as one big event where Israel becomes the chief of the nations and God reigns through their earthly king. Surely Jesus is about to call on some angel armies and take over from both the Romans and the power-hungry Jewish leaders! Today, maybe?

Now we're ready to start with our first KEY PASSAGE: Matthew 24.

They've spent the day in the temple; Jesus was busy helping people, teaching those who would listen, and exchanging strong words with the Jewish leaders. Now it's time to spend the evening in peace and quiet in the olive grove across the valley.

But first, the disciples just have to get Jesus to stop focusing on people and notice the *stuff*. The temple was their people's pride and joy. It had taken generations to build, much like the cathedrals of Europe would long after.

Jesus, of course, had seen the temple, and he blows their minds by pointing out its coming fate. At some point, nothing would be left intact.

Hearing this horrifying news, the disciples can't help asking about it when they reach their destination and sit down where they could all see the gold and stonework gleam in the last rays of the sun. They ask two KEY questions:

- When will the temple be thrown down?
- What is the sign that Jesus is returning and of the end of the age?

For the rest of this chapter and the next Jesus answers them, and it's not a cozy bedtime story he tells.

First, he warns them to watch out. Many are going to lie, trying to get them to believe they are the Messiah. Sadly, Jesus predicts it's going to work on a lot of people.

You know what the news sells? Alarm, fright, worry. Bad things happening all over the place. And bad things are always happening. Nations fight, rulers throw each other out of power, pandemics, earthquakes, and famines wipe out vast numbers of people—but these tragedies don't mean it's time for the end.

Verse 8 talks about the "beginning of sorrows" or "birth pangs." When a woman is going to have a baby, her body starts getting the muscles ready to push him out long before it's time to go to the hospital. Ask your mom about this. These squeezes aren't fun, but they don't usually hurt much and they can happen for months before things get serious.

Now I've got a question for you. Who asked Jesus the questions that got him started? Who does he warn will be hated by every nation, arrested, given a hard time, and killed? This isn't some splintered-off group of Jesus's followers leaving the rest of us in peace. This is normal treatment for all of Jesus's people everywhere at all times. If it's not happening to you right now be thankful, but don't get soft.

Oh, yes, in **verse 9** see the word "afflicted" (or your Bible might have "punished," or "persecuted")? This is a KEY word for understanding both our experience now and what will happen to people in the future. Some translations use a word we hear about a lot in End Times teaching: "tribulation."

We are used to thinking this is one terrible event in future history, but in **John 16:33** Jesus told his disciples that all his followers would experience this. In the New Testament, there are dozens of places where we are either told tribulation will happen or was happening to Jesus's people. Bad guys can experience tribulation too, but if you look up *Strong's* #2347 you'll see how often it happens to Jesus's people both then and throughout time.

In **verse 10** it talks about being "offended" or "falling away." The idea is to get tripped up. If you are running and something trips you, you might end up heading in a totally different direction. **Psalm 119:165** talks about how following the Bible protects you from stumbling like this.

Uncomfortable as it is, Jesus warned us that being betrayed and hated because of our love of Jesus is normal. During World War II, Corrie Ten Boom's family was betrayed by a neighbor to the German police for money and it is still happening today in many countries.

Didn't Jesus already tell us people will try to get us to believe lies before **verse 11**? He gave us two truth-witnesses in a single passage!

A false prophet is someone who tells people they are sharing God's message, either about the future or just what God thinks is important and good. They tell people what they want to hear rather than what God really wants. No wonder so many people are going to listen; it's going to be hard even for believers not to fall for their pleasant words.

Verse 12 is a spot where we can see how brilliant Jesus is. Remember, this is the same Creator who made DNA, so, this verse could mean other people's sin makes a Christian bitter at God or at people. It can also mean Christians will be tempted to sin themselves and end up forgetting Jesus or other people. It probably means all this and more!

Some people believe a person can truly belong to Jesus for a time but then do something so bad they still end up in hell. **Verse 13** sounds like the kind of thing you would point to if this is true. So, let's think about it:

If I belong to Jesus, will he help me hold on to him to the end? If he can, I don't need to worry, but I do need to hold on. Jesus loving me no matter what doesn't mean I'm allowed to be lazy, believe everything I hear, and hurt people. Living like Jesus wants me to is hard work, even when I know he's helping me do it.

Back when your grandparents weren't even born yet, missionaries read **verse 14** and wanted to help clear the way for Jesus's kingdom. They dedicated their lives to finding people groups without the Bible in their own language and telling them about Jesus. Every year more Bibles are printed in new languages where no one had ever heard about Jesus until just a few years ago.

A pivot point

You're going to see this again in other passages, so let's think this through. If you are walking along in one direction and realize you need to turn a corner, you can do this by swinging your body around while one foot stays still. Or you might grab a pole and swing around as you race in a new direction.

This is what the end of **verse 14** does. It swings us from the long, regular history of Jesus's people to the time of "the end." You'll see this right away in the next verse.

Jesus expects those who hear him to see something called the "abomination of desolation." And he tells us Daniel is the prophet who predicted that this object will get set up. We'll look at what it is as soon as we finish studying Jesus's prophecy. Now Jesus adds what to do when this thing shows up—run!

Have you seen pictures of the kinds of houses people had in Bible times? The roofs were like a big patio and the way you went up and down was built into the outside. To grab something from the ground floor, you had to go down the stairs and then inside. It wasn't like our houses where the stairs are usually in the middle.

Everything about Jesus's warning points to how urgent their need to escape is going to be. If they even take a few seconds to grab a blanket, their lives are in danger. That's as scary as a flash flood or tsunami warning.

Did you know that Jesus showed extraordinary care for women and people with physical limitations? Even as he's picturing the distant future, he's thinking about how rough it will be for women with babies. Their bodies are weak and those tiny lives depend on things staying calm.

In World War II a missionary named Darlene Deibler Rose was captured in Indonesia. She then was moved to a prison cell with nothing inside but a cement floor, but God had guided her to wear the one dress she owned that had a full enough skirt to use as a blanket. He didn't make the trial go away, but he provided for it not to be as horrible as it could have been.

~

And for all of us, let's think about what Jesus is telling us it's OK to pray for. Hard times come to us as Christians. But Jesus wants us to pray that it won't be the worst possible conditions. Winter is muddy and chilly in Israel. The Sabbath there has extra travel restrictions. God likes it when we ask for help to survive the trials he brings into our lives.

We've already seen that this word "distress" or "tribulation" is used often about the hard times we go through. The only difference in **verse 21** is that here Jesus calls it a time of "great" or "mega" (that's what the Greek word is) pressure. And he has already told us who is in big trouble: the people who follow him. It's going to be a time so terrible nothing like it has ever happened before and it will only be allowed to happen once. And it's not going to last as long as it could have.

The word "shortened" in **verse 22** means to "cut off," like you might lop off the arm of a statue. It's a serious word! You'll need to remember this when we start calculating the timeframe for the end of history as we know it. Because Jesus said these days of affliction won't last as long as they could have.

We know it is God who shortens these days because only he has the power to determine how long an experience is supposed to last. And he cares about people's lives, especially his "elect." Unlike the people we vote for, "elect" here means the ones God has picked out. Anyone who ends up in heaven gets there because God chose them and wanted them. And he cares when we are dying from terrible trials!

Didn't Jesus already warn us not to fall for lies? **Verses 23–24** make the 3rd time he's warned us about false prophets. I think this might be a major issue when it's time for Jesus to come back, don't you?

But this isn't just the same warning about the same pleasant fakeness. This time they are trying to convince us Christ is on earth and you could go visit him. They will even do mega miracles to prove they are right. Those of us who are chosen by God and trust Jesus are going to know they must be fakes, but it's going to be hard to resist their claims. If we didn't have Jesus's warning already, we would fall for them.

Verse 27 starts the next and last section of Jesus's timeline for The End. We don't have to go searching for the Christ; it's going to be as obvious as a giant lightning flash. And this bright sign is going to be Jesus, the Son of Man, himself.

You can find good scholars who believe all kinds of opposite things about Jesus's claim here. Some think the carcass is the Jews and the vultures are God's judgments. Others think the carcass is the gospel and the vultures are new Christians. Still others think the carcass is Jesus and the vultures are his people collecting to him.

Interestingly, in **Luke 17:37** Jesus gives a variation of his prediction that ties the birds and dead body analogy to some people being taken and others left. Assuming both times Jesus is using the birds in the same way, it makes the last option the most likely. And it also fits other puzzle pieces we're about to see.

Verses 29–31 form the most important KEY to the future in the whole Bible. If you get this right, the rest falls into place easily and comfortably. Get these verses wrong, and the future stays a muddy muddle. Let's get them right, shall we!

Following right after the mega trouble for Jesus's people comes a truly amazing sign in the heavens. The sun and moon stop shining and the stars fall. We will see this event talked about in a bunch of places all over the Bible. And what happens before and after these signs changes everything about how we see God's predictions of the future.

The "powers of heaven" (or "heavenly bodies") are not something we can know what Jesus is talking about for sure, but it is fascinating to think about. There are powerful physical forces like gravity that affect outer space, but there are also spiritual forces shaping history and controlling countries. Jesus could have easily meant both the physical and spiritual powers will be shaken here.

At this time what will show up in the dark heavens? The "sign" of Jesus, the Son of Man, in heaven. He won't be on earth like the false prophets were claiming; he's going to be up in the sky. And it isn't going to make the Earth Dwellers—the people whose only citizenship is this world—happy. They will be horrified as they watch Jesus's glory and power. Jesus is no sissy, and although we'll have to look at other Scriptures to find out what he is capable of, we can already tell from here he is one scary dude. You do *not* want him for your enemy!

But at first Jesus doesn't do anything deadly. Instead, he sends his angels out with a "mega" trumpet (think Jesus likes using that word?) to do something. He sends them out to find his chosen in every part of the earth, no matter how far away they are. Their job is to gather them together.

Most likely you have heard that this event is called "the Rapture," but if you haven't, we'll save it for when we study 1 Thessalonians. Just don't forget, this is how the tribulation of God's elect gets "cut off" since it's kinda hard to torment people that get gathered to Jesus in the heavens by an angel.

So, to review, if you get Jesus's prophecy here right, you've got the keys to unlocking the future. You need:

The trouble, the sign, the Son, the clouds, the power and glory, the fear, and the gathering!

Jesus gives us another pivot point in **verse 32**. In fact, except for the parable of the sheep and goat judgment in the next chapter, he doesn't give us any new events from this point on. Instead, he's going to circle back around to how we should think as the time gets closer and closer. And first he starts with how obvious these events will be for his people if they pay attention.

Just like you can watch the trees grow greener every day when the last frost has ended, so we will be able to see things getting ready for the last great trial of God's people and Jesus's coming in glory.

Anyone who tells you there is nothing we can watch for and that Jesus could come back any day out of the clear blue sky hasn't taken Jesus's warning here seriously. Even if they are a pastor who writes books and makes movies. Period.

Verse 34 is a favorite for those who want to say all these events happened back when General Titus destroyed Jerusalem and the temple in 70 AD. And it is the strongest verse they have. But does it have to mean the people who were alive when Jesus was had to still be alive when the prophecy was fulfilled?

Although some translations jump straight to having Jesus talk about "people alive now," the original word for this is "generation." So, let's look at how the Bible uses this idea. First, turn back to **Proverbs 30:11–14**. Were these people only around at one point in history and there's never been anyone like them ever again? Would it make more sense to see these people as a 'class' of similar people who have been around since Cain and there are still plenty of them around today?

One of the KEYS to all of God's working with his people, especially when they refuse to obey him is the song God had Moses teach the Israelis just before he died. **Deuteronomy 32:1–43** was all prophecy when it was recorded, but the history of the descendants of Jacob shows how real God's warnings and promises have held true. **Verse 5** was a favorite for Jesus to quote to the Pharisees, but was Moses only predicting a single group of people born during the quarter-century right before the change from BC to AD?

Philippians 2:15 uses this same word "generation." Can you find it? Does Paul mean only the people around when he wrote to this church had neighbors like that?

In Mark 8:38 Jesus warned his disciples that anyone who was ashamed of him and his words in "this sinful generation" would embarrass Jesus when he comes with the angels in his father's glory. Does this mean only those living at the time of Christ live with an evil generation?

Of course, generation *can* mean the same thing as Baby Boomer or Millennial. But even these titles mean more than just a person born at a certain time; they tell us about the attitudes and values of many of those people.

So, unless we can find other verses that tell us we *have to* expect all these prophecies to be totally fulfilled during the lifetimes of those alive with Jesus, this verse isn't enough by itself.

Verse 35 doesn't tell us anything new, but it does tell us something foundationally important. We can trust Jesus to give us the real scoop. He said it; we can stake our lives on it actually happening.

Here's a million-dollar question to ask someone who thinks the Rapture happens out of the blue. First, ask them which Bible verse tells us we don't know when the Rapture happens. Odds are good they will point to **Matthew 24:36**. But then ask them where in this passage Jesus tells us what "that day and hour" is. They won't be able to find it. But you can, right? It's only a couple of verses earlier (Hint: remember, I told you those verses were the keys to all of prophecy.).

Look again at the fig tree in verse 32; Jesus tells us we can know the "season" as things mature towards this day and hour. All we can't be sure of is the exact timing.

And Jesus telling us even he doesn't know the calendar day and time! This gives us an amazing hint into Jesus's manhood. Somehow, at least while he was living on earth, he limited himself to what his human brain could handle, so details like this only the Father kept.

Verses 37–41 form a set around the timing of the coming of the Son of Man. So, all of them have to do with the things that change in verse 30.

It's interesting to see how some people want to believe Jesus is really going to come back and judge the whole world but they don't want to believe God already did judge the whole world with one event in the past. Jesus tells us his return will have a lot of similarities to Noah's experience.

Here's an unexpected KEY to the End Times. See what **verses 38–39** tell us about the people who were shocked when judgment fell? It wasn't God's people—Noah had known it was coming for ages. It was the wicked. Their lives went on uninterrupted until the very Day of Judgment. Jesus tells us this is exactly how it's going to be when he comes again.

When people have decided verse 31 doesn't have to do with Jesus rescuing his people, they have some interesting ideas about **verses 40–41**. They will point to how Noah 'escaped' from the flood a full week before it started (Genesis 7:1–4), forgetting to mention that while they moved in then, they weren't shut inside until the very day the flood started (Genesis 7:13–16).

Then they need to explain the people going about their daily work and what happens to them. Instead of seeing the ones "taken" as being rescued, they see them being removed from their homeland for judgment.

In Luke 17:26–37, Jesus talks about the same thing. First, he brings in the oblivious people of Noah's day, then he talks about Lot being the only one warned about the destruction of Sodom, then he talks about escaping. He even mentioned the people doing their work and adds that some workers will be in their bunk sleeping at the time this happens.

Both times, while Jesus has talked about the righteous being pulled away from coming doom, he didn't give us any hint that the people minding their own business are pulled away from their honest work to be judged as wicked. Instead, those left in Noah's and Lot's situations were the ones judged. If you didn't need to see people taken to judgment to keep your theology, you would never think that was Jesus's meaning.

Verse 42–44 set us another puzzle. Understand this KEY and you'll have a lot straightened out. Leave it a riddle and you'll be stuck.

Jesus tells us to keep watch because he isn't going to tell us the exact time he is coming back. He even tells us he can't be more specific because there's someone else who would figure too much out if he did.

And that someone is a "master" of a house who will find Jesus comes to him as a thief. It's this master who will have Jesus take all his stuff away at an unexpected time.

We will see Jesus being compared to a thief again soon, but here, can you figure out who he "robs"? There has been someone in charge of the world as a whole since the dawn of time. In **Matthew 12:25–29**, Jesus is telling off the Pharisees for claiming he was using satanic power to throw out demons. In the last verse, he uses this exact analogy and tells us you can't take stuff away from a strongman who has control over a household until you first tie up the strongman.

From Genesis 3 on, we know that Satan has power over the world in a way that is not good for God's people. We'll be seeing a lot more of what he's been up to in the Book of Revelation and beyond. God's worst enemy gets around.

From this point through the end of **chapter 25** we get much more general stories and warnings about the conditions leading up to the Coming of the Son of Man. You'll want to read it, but I won't take you through verse by verse.

Here are a handful of things to notice on your way through:

- **Verses 50–51** This ruler of Jesus's people (that would be some sort of pastor or church authority) does not recognize the signs of Jesus's return, and he gets sent to hell. Not everyone with "Christian" next to their name is going to see what's going on, and Jesus sure won't let them get away with their rotten behavior.
- **Chapter 25 verses 8–12** Whatever the oil is, it will have run down during the wait. No one can share with another, we all need our own, and without it you cannot enter Jesus's kingdom. Waiting until you already need a 2nd dose of oil will doom some to not belonging to Jesus at all.
- **Verses 14–30** give us a version of the parable of the talents we don't read as often as Luke's (19:14–27). God has every right to give some people an "unfair" advantage in life. He makes it fair by rewarding us based on what we do with what each of us is given, whether it was a lot or a little. All those who enter the joy of their master get the same reward. But the servant who thought he knew how mean the master was, gets thrown into hell. He refused to honor God with the things life gave him.
- The story of the Sheep and Goat judgment puzzles some people. They wonder whether it happens when Jesus first becomes king or when it's time for the very last mortal people to enter eternity. **Verse 31** tells us this happens when the Son of Man comes with his angels. That makes it pretty clear it happens sooner rather than later.
- Both the good and bad people didn't realize the choices they were making at the time. They did what they chose to do and only later found out how much it mattered to Jesus. The Bible is full of times when God cares deeply about the sick and miserable. Jesus's life was filled with helping such people out. And the New Testament reminds us to pay attention to the needy. **Galatians 2:10** tells us this was something of highest importance to the early church, and James, the main pastor of Jerusalem, tells us this is how you can tell someone really cares about following God in **James 1:27**. Can someone help a poor person for selfish reasons? Sure, although probably not much when it becomes unpopular. But if you care about God, you are guaranteed to also care about his suffering people.

Mark and Luke's Versions of Jesus's Prophecy

There are good reasons to start with Matthew, and it's not just because it comes first in the Bible. Mark 13 has nearly the same account as Matthew, just a little shorter. Go ahead and read it though, since seeing it repeated helps us remember just how important Jesus thought this was. And pay attention to how **verses 24–26** mention basically the same details about the Sign of the Coming of the Son of Man.

Luke has a rather different focus though. Let's walk through it:

Luke 21:5–36

Do you see how the disciples ask a slightly different question in **verse 7** from what Matthew reports? Their question and Jesus's response are much more focused on the 1st Century temple and its destruction.

Matthew 10:16–28 also talks about God helping us out when we are forced to testify before judges and rulers, and how Jesus's people will be persecuted from city to city even by our families. Jesus probably repeated himself rather often during his years of teaching on earth to make sure his disciples absorbed his message. But here in Luke 21, it isn't just a general prediction of the Christian life, it's a prophecy about Jerusalem.

Verse 18 seems to be the opposite of **verse 16**. How can you have not even a hair be destroyed if your whole body is being killed? As we'll study soon, what happens to a Christian when we die? We get a new, forever body that cannot be harmed. God will watch over every part of us that matters: our souls and spirits. This helps us calm down from the worry of losing our grip on Jesus. He's got us—even our hair!

Verses 20–24 show us just how different this prophecy is from Matthew. Had we seen armies before? No. Do we see an "abomination" here? No. Even the "time of vengeance" is new. The beginning of verse 24 couldn't be easier to understand; it is clearly talking about the destruction of the temple and Jerusalem in 70 AD by the Roman army.

But why are verses 21 and 23 so similar to Matthew's version then?

Remember how prophecy forms a drawing on a stack of paper. The same picture can be seen on several sheets. Luke's version up to this point has been tightly focused on the near events of what would happen in Jerusalem to God's Jewish people.

And here's what's cool. Early church records tell us every single known Christian living in Jerusalem obeyed Jesus's warning. They got out and not one was killed by the Romans at that time. But they didn't get out with the help of angels and trumpets gathering them to Jesus, they fled to towns across the Jordan.

Verse 24 forms another pivot post. See how Jesus tells them the fate of Jerusalem after its destruction? He says it will be controlled by the world's peoples until the "times of the Gentiles" were finished up. Remember this, you'll need this KEY when we get to Daniel.

Surprisingly, there are only five verses left of Jesus's prediction here. And he swings straight to what his people would care about most. The very next verse after Jerusalem's downfall mentions the signs in the sun, moon, and stars! It adds how confused and terrified the nations (and oceans) are at this point, and then moves right on to the Son of Man showing up in the clouds.

The one new bit Luke adds for those alive at the time of Jesus's glorious return is that, when these particular signs finally happen, it is time for Jesus's people to raise our heads and watch for him.

Daniel and the 70th Week

Now that we have looked at Jesus's main predictions about coming events, it's time to look at the prophet he expected us to have read and understood.

The book of Daniel divides neatly into two sections: highlights from the events of Daniel's life and a collection of visions he was given about the future. Since the first dream, Nebuchadnezzar was given in chapter 2 was also a prophecy, there's rather a lot of the book for us to study!

Let's start with this dream of the metallic statue.

It's a fairly long chapter, but makes for an exciting story. What had so angered the king? Why did his executioner listen to Daniel instead of killing him right then? How did Daniel manage to fall asleep knowing he and his friends were doomed without God's help?

But what we are interested in is the way the statue gives us a glimpse into world history. Daniel starts out in **verse 32** by telling Nebuchadnezzar that his own rule was the golden head. It's a straightforward thing from there to assemble the next few empires that take over both the area of Babylon and particularly the land of Israel.

After Babylon came the Medes and Persians during Daniel's own lifetime. Then Alexander the Great brought the power of the Greeks to the East. Finally, the Romans took over, not only the whole Mediterranean but all the way to the border of Persia. They never got a stronghold in the area of Iran because the Persians were too good at fighting on horseback.

But then something started to break the power of the Romans. Was it another even stronger empire? No, the empire fell to a "death by a thousand paper cuts." The empire was simply too big to hold together without a strong leader and immense army.

Changes in Roman culture and pressure from lots of Germanic tribes sweeping in from the north made it harder for the army to keep any kind of peace. As time went on, most of the soldiers fighting for Rome were actually Germans. Eventually, the empire was split into two sections, the western one sinking into just another city-state even though they tried all kinds of treaties (including marriages as Daniel predicted), but the eastern one with its capital in Byzantium lasted for another thousand years.

And something else was quietly happening all over the empire. A new allegiance was making more and more people unwilling to think Rome had the right to rule over everyone else or that being a soldier was the highest calling. It not only infected the Roman citizens, it changed the priorities and actions of the tribes around them too.

Even though Christianity has often been only a name for the leaders of government across Europe, Jesus's kingdom has never been thrown down like Rome was; not even the Islamic empire was able to snuff it out. In spite of the rise and fall of individual countries, Jesus's gospel has spread everywhere. Nebuchadnezzar's dream still leaves room for a final fulfillment at the end of history—like, why did Daniel mention *toes?*—but it has already been fulfilled in a global way.

This is only one example of Daniel's keystone prophecies. Let's move on to his future and ours.

Daniel 7

We just finished reading about the empire statue. Now we get to read about the empire animals. Watch how closely the characteristics of the gold, silver, bronze, and iron line up with the first vision. And here we start to get more details about these kingdoms.

The winged lion standing up looks almost exactly like the winged door guardians of Ashurnasirpal II, who lived several centuries before Daniel, which you can visit in the Berlin Museum. The bear being much higher on one side than the other fits with the off-kilter power between the Medes (weaker) and the Persians (stronger). Today, conservationists are trying to preserve the few Persian bears that still live in Iran.

The Greeks connected their god of wine and insanity with the leopard, and our word panther is the ancient Greek word for these creatures. See how this creature has four wings and four heads in **verse 6**? You can study this more, but we know when Alexander the Great died, his four generals divided up his empire and took over.

The "terrible" animal that shows up last isn't compared to a real-world animal like the others. All we know about its appearance is its teeth in **verse 7**. Remember what the legs and feet of Nebuchadnezzar's statue were made out of? This one doesn't have teeth of iron by accident.

Now we learn more about those still future ten leaders. It starts out as ten, but it doesn't stay that way. While seven remain, three get uprooted by a "little horn." And this Little Horn has a mouth on him, speaking great, or powerful, things. We are going to be seeing this guy a lot more.

In Daniel's vision, the next thing that happens is the Ancient of Days taking over and handing the eternal kingdom to the Son of Man. You'll see in **verses 11–12** what happens to the world empires after God takes over. The iron-tooth beast and its mouthy horn get killed and tossed in the fire. But the other creatures are left alive for a season.

Here's where things get really interesting. In the Hebrew mind horns were symbols of power and dignity. When you read the Psalms (75:4,5; 89:17,24; 92:10; 112:9, etc.) you see horns being lifted up. Both Samuel's mom (1 Samuel 2:1) and John the Baptist's dad (Luke 1:69) mention horns being "exalted." So, Daniel wanted to know more about this mouthy horn, and he *is* shown more. **Verse 19** up to the end of the chapter walks us through understanding this Little Horn more closely.

We learn that although this horn is small, it *looked greater* than the rest. Then **verse 21** is scary. This Little Horn fights a war, a war against God's holy people, or saints. Not only this, he keeps winning against them. Ahh! But God puts a stop to him and flips the tables so the saints end up deciding the fate of the Little Horn and take over the kingdom.

Verse 23 circles around a third time to the last beast and Daniel learns it will rule over the whole earth, breaking it "in pieces."

Then in **verse 25**, we find out some important details about the Little Horn. He not only talks a big talk, he's talking smack about God himself. He will "wear out," or treat, God's saints horribly. And he will attempt to change how time is measured as well as the law code.

At several points in history, we've had countries that tried to change how time is measured. The atheistic French Revolution introduced a ten-day week, and the Soviet Union tried several different workweek cycles that didn't line up with the seven-day week. It's fascinating that among the many laws the Little Horn isn't going to keep, the way *time* is measured is one of them.

It is even possible that he will reset the year to no longer tie to when Jesus was born as it does today, much like the Muslims measure their years back to the founding of Islam rather than Christianity.

Now we get one more of the main KEYS to how events play out at the end of history. Reread the end of **verse 25**. See that "time, times, and half a time"? This is one of the main ways to measure how long it takes to move from the Little Horn ruling the world to when Jesus becomes king of everything forever!

If all we had was this verse we couldn't be clear about what these 1+2+1/2 units mean, but we're going to see this set over and over. And they break out to equal a three and a half year period. This is all the time the Little Horn is given for his kingdom, but we've seen how powerful he is during this blip in history.

Like Daniel, all this stuff can really bother our brains. It's not fun to think of all this evil coming before God and his people take over.

I'm going to leave off a lot of the rest of Daniel's prophecies. They are amazing, but much of it already happened. A cool point is that, when Alexander the Great reached Jerusalem, the priests welcomed him as the leopard of Daniel and he left them alone since they had predicted his success.

Daniel 8

Much of chapter 8 has to do with the Greek Ptolemies of Egypt. Interestingly, although this empire was part of the Greeks, which were the leopard in the last chapter, we get to see the Little Horn at work again. **Verses 9–14** talk about what this Greek version, or type, does.

We can only guess at the spiritual powers knocking down stars and taking on the "prince of the host." But watch what he does in Jerusalem, the "pleasant land." He takes away the sacrifices, throws truth to the ground, and becomes hugely successful.

Verse 13 describes what the Little Horn does as a "transgression" or "rebellion" that brings desolation. Remember Jesus mentioning this?

Next, we are given a timeline of 2,300 days. Since this prophecy is already fulfilled, it doesn't need to fit neatly into a prophetic calendar (where a year equals 360 days). It could mean the 6+ year period Antiochus Epiphanes persecuted the Jews. It could mean 2,300 evenings and mornings, marking a smaller time when this Greek ruler set up a statue of himself in the Temple of God.

Daniel 9

I will never forget the first time my family read this chapter as we were reading our way through the Old Testament. Daniel's prayer and the reason he prayed it blew me away. Here was a man who had followed God and been blessed by him like few others in history. Yet his words are so passionate as he makes his case for God to forgive and hear him even though he was part of a wayward people.

The prophecy may not start until toward the end of the chapter, but we are wise to get our hearts in tune with Daniel's first, so we are ready to hear from God with the same amazement and faith.

Then, in **verse 21**, things start to get really interesting. The messenger God sends with his prediction is the same guy who would one day show up to both Zechariah and Mary to talk about some babies coming to transform history.

That's quite an interesting job he got.

And Gabriel lets Daniel in on a bit of the viewpoint of heaven. God really, really loves Daniel. That doesn't mean God plays favorites, this is why we started at the beginning of the chapter. Who wouldn't greatly love someone who worshipped and honored you the way Daniel did from his youth? And each of us can be this special to God too.

So, because of God's love for Daniel, he gives him one of the biggest KEYS to the future anyone ever got. If you understand **verse 24**, you've got the main timeline for all prophecy. What we have to do is answer a few questions:

- How much time is this going to take?
- Who and where is the full prophecy focused on?

The "Seventy Weeks of Daniel" is the most famous timeframe in all prophecy, but no one thinks this means 490 days. That would force all of these prophecies to be fulfilled before there was time for more than collecting the first group of exiles to return to the ruins of Jerusalem. Instead, we assume each "day" equals a year.

And these 490 years give us the length of time required for a whole list of things to happen to both Daniel's people, the Jews, and the holy city, Jerusalem.

1. To put a wrap on transgression (crossing God's line into evil)
2. To end sin
3. To forgive iniquity
4. To seal the vision and prophecy
5. To anoint the most holy place

How many of these have already happened? The first three fit beautifully into the purpose of Jesus's first coming as our Redeemer from sin, but what about the other two? Can you see how a lot of what the Messiah (Jesus) was going to do didn't get finished with his death and return to heaven? And, while this verse fits pretty comfortably with the thinking that all prophecy wrapped up in 70 AD, it doesn't *have to* mean it. And what about the most holy place? It didn't get "anointed" by anyone back then. It got destroyed!

Verse 25 *was* prophecy, but it's now history. We know Cyrus commanded to rebuild the temple and Nehemiah was allowed to rebuild the walls. When we assume each 'day' of these 69 weeks is a year, you come out pretty neatly to the time of Jesus's earthly ministry. Although scholars vary a handful of years on when to start the count and where you end up in Jesus's life, if you go back to 483 years before 30 A.D. you come out smack dab in the middle of when Nehemiah was governor over Judah.

Hold your place in Daniel and turn to Jesus's lament over Jerusalem in **Luke 19:42**. What did he mourn that they didn't know? Can you see why it should have been easy for them to spot the timeframe when God would be visiting?

Verse 26 is a whiplash-inducing pivot point. First, you have the Messiah (Jesus) cut off. Jewish people who can't picture their Messiah being crucified, like the real one was, have to do some fancy explaining on this one. Then it swings instantly to the destruction of Jerusalem but throws in the "people" of the "prince" who is to come, or the "entering prince." The desolations that are decreed seem to go with the temple never being restored from that point on.

This carries us right on to the one remaining week of Gabriel's 70 weeks. And what happens then is spelled out in **verse 27**. First, we need to know who "he" is. Some people want it to be Jesus and how he was the Jewish Messiah, but, since the Jews didn't accept him he was no longer bound to them anymore. But one of the rules for studying pronouns is to tie it with the noun closest to it. And the closest here is the "prince" whose people destroy the city.

Let's see what happens when we assume this interpretation:

- He makes an agreement with many people for seven years.
- He no longer allows offerings and sacrifices after 3½ years.
- Then he sets up the abomination of desolation.
- But God will destroy the destroyer.

Have we seen some of this in other prophecies? Yes, and we're going to see it again.

Daniel 11

Daniel 10 is one of the coolest passages in the whole Bible; you don't want to miss the way angels have to fight in the real world! But the prophecy Gabriel gets through to Daniel has all happened already up to about **11:35**. Go ahead and read it, watching for how even the worst actors don't have the way greased for them. Throughout history, the bad guys only get their way by lying, bribing, and such underhanded things.

We've seen this in recent years with the Soviets struggling against those who wanted freedom, Hitler only seizing power by making secret arrangements with people behind closed doors, and dictators cheating when they hold an election to hold on to their power. Even in countries that have never followed God on purpose, evil people have to be sneaky and mean to get the power they crave.

Verse 35 is still talking about the now-historical conditions during the time of Antiochus Epiphanies and the Maccabees. But we've seen this same pivot point phrase before. Can you spot it? Yes, it mentions "until the time of the end." This is the same way Jesus put it. So, let's see what happens when we assume everything from this point on hasn't happened yet.

This king in **verse 36**. Does he remind you of a character we've seen already in Daniel? Especially how mouthy he is? It's fascinating to see this dude is successful until the time of being seriously angry is completed. And there is a time set aside just for this guy to have his way.

Verse 37 really fires up the imaginations of some people. But we see people like this all the time in our culture. The only thing this verse tells us is this guy is an atheist and a humanist. He makes himself his own highest authority. And there are tons of people like this today; the only difference is this guy is getting others to agree *he* is the top of the heap.

Well, perhaps he isn't a normal atheist who worships science. **Verse 38** tells us this king worships a "god of fortresses" or as the KJV and International Children's Bible put it "forces" or "strength." Whatever he honors, it's pretty much just something that gives him strength, like a fort gives an army a "stronghold." It's clear this isn't a normal Zeus-and-Baal idol though, a fortress doesn't have a personality—or even a body.

This same word for fortresses shows up in **verse 39**, where he's placing his treasure gifts in different fortresses. And look why he does it—so his gifts and the god it represents can rule over many. Well, if you're reading anything besides the KJV you are going to read that it's the people who help him take over the fortresses whom he will honor and make rulers. I wouldn't want to be a Bible translator for anything, because there is probably room for both of these interpretations to work, but they have to pick only one.

Verses 40–45 don't read like anything else in End Times prophecy. We've seen it in Daniel already, though about the now historical rulers of Ptolemy Egypt. Basically, this fortress-worshipping king doesn't have it all his way. He's got rulers from both the north and the south pushing against him. And he's going to send his armies flowing over the "glorious" land (Israel) but not through their neighbors just east of the Jordan River. He plunders Egypt and settles in a palace in Israel. But his end is coming.

Daniel 12

This is one spot where the chapter breaks don't make any sense. It's pretty obvious verse 1 of Daniel 12 fits right up next to verse 45 of the last chapter. So, let's keep reading!

Right when it's time for this fortress-god king to meet his demise, Michael the archangel shows up. And it's not pretty.

Daniel tells us there will be a time of trouble like never before in history. Does anyone else tell us about a time like this? Yes, Jesus does. And it happens when a powerful king is out to get God's people. Daniel, of course, is focused on his own Jewish family, and that's what we see here. The Jewish people are going to escape, or slip away like a greased, umm, fish from the harm that king wanted to do to them.

Verses 2–3 add something we hadn't seen before with prophecy, but we're going to see it again. Tied right in with the godly Jewish people escaping the worst persecution of all time comes a massive resurrection. Daniel's version is interesting because it points out that both good and bad people will be raised.

This does not have to mean all these people come alive at the same moment in time. Remember, prophetic pictures are often multi-layered with distant events spoken of right next to each other. We'll have to look at other prophecies to find out the timing, but what we get here is that the resurrection is coming and is somehow tied to this escape of the godly Jews.

Lots of people have fun imagining what Gabriel means in **verse 4**. They could be right, but just because we live in an age when we can share information through the internet like no generation before us does not mean the end has to come right now. And the beginning of the verse tells us it's not going to be easy to try to make sense of the prophecy; it's been "sealed."

Verse 5 opens the last scene in Daniel's book. He is witness to some angels asking and answering questions. It's interesting to catch a glimpse of how some angels know things other angels don't—or, didn't—know.

The riverbank angels ask the linen waterman how long all these prophecies are going to take. And the answer is a serious one, promised to happen by God's own life. These events will take 3 1/2 "times" to be finished.

It isn't fun to realize God is going to allow his people to have their ability to resist evil completely "shattered." We wish he would just let us win all the time! But we'll find out soon why God lets so much evil happen to us first (Hint: in 2 Thessalonians 1 and Revelation 6).

We saw Jesus telling us something a lot like what we read in **verse 10**. Here God is, wanting his people prepared for the difficulty they will face, but he also knows Satan is perfectly capable of reading the Bible too. He did it in Eden, he did it to Jesus in Matthew 4:6. So, God had to tell us how things are going to play out in a way that all the bad guys won't catch on.

Verses 11–12 give us another specific-to-the-day timeline to expect. We already know the Abomination of Desolation and taking away the daily sacrifice are connected. This passage tells us straight up they happen at the same time. And you can count from that very day to when the earthly reign of Jesus begins in earnest. Interestingly, a three and a half year period would be only 1,260 days. Why there are an extra 45 days tacked on is something total prophecy geeks like to puzzle over, but I'm not going to tackle it here.

And, just to wrap things up with an encouraging bow, Daniel is told in the last verse that after a lovely rest from his hardworking life, he'll get to be there when the end comes. And if *he* does, so will all of God's people who have wondered about these things ever since.

Odds and Ends leading up to Revelation

We would be stumped trying to put together a picture of prophecy without the long passages we've been looking at, but some of the shorter passages scattered around give us hints and glimmers of what will happen that help us understand the big sections even better.

These bits can be found all over the place, so get your Bible drill skills ready for some quick flipping!

The Great Prophecy

Let's go all the way back to the beginning. Genesis 3 marks the transfer of power over the earth from Adam (who was given dominion in Genesis 1:28) to Satan. It doesn't say exactly what happened here, but **Romans 6:16** tells us we become servants of whomever we obey. When Adam followed his wife and ate the fruit God told him not to, but Satan *had* told him to, he became subject to Satan. At that point, Satan had a new home territory—everything Adam had been given—and that covered the whole world.

In **Genesis 3:15** humans were given their first prophecy. God actually told it directly to the snake, but Adam and Eve were listening in. He was told a "seed of the woman" would crush his head after he had crushed his heel. The word for what the snake does is the same as what happens to the woman's seed, but I'd rather have my heel damaged than my head!

This prophecy also tells us two things about the one who will smash Satan's head. He is a human, but because of his mother, not his father. Only one human being has ever been the "seed of the woman." And this is why anyone who claims Jesus had an ordinary human dad is not a proper Christian. The Holy Spirit is the one who took Mary's human egg and added the genetic information needed for her to bear a sinless but human son.

Old Testament Prophecies about the Day of the Lord

If you look up the phrase "day of the Lord" in the KJV, you'll find those exact words used 29 times, all but 5 in the Old Testament. Many of these are double prophecies with a near fulfillment long before Jesus was born and only bits looking all the way to the end of history.

Let's take a look at some of the more interesting ones:

Isaiah 2:12−22 says God's day will affect the proud. Verse 17 says it straight up: only God will be exalted in that day. And verses 19−21 give us a glimpse into how the proud will hide themselves and their idols in caves.

Isaiah 13 has its near fulfillment in the conquering of Babylon, but it's important to remember that when the Medes and Persians took over during Daniel's lifetime the transition was nearly bloodless. Even Daniel, who was third in the last Babylonian king's government, just moves from serving one ruler to another. Many of these predictions look ridiculous if we force them to only mean the past.

- Verse 9: Tells us it is the LORD's day of wrath. Who is in trouble during this time?
- Verse 10: Have we seen these signs before? When does Jesus tell us these fit in?
- Verse 11: Does this line up with Jesus's timeline in Matthew 24?

In verse 20 we are told no one will ever live in Babylon again. In Daniel's day, the city changed leadership but it continued to be lived in. Although it slowly sank into decay, even today a handful of people live in Nebuchadnezzar's old capital. We'll see this same prediction of the complete desolation of this city again!

Isaiah 34 is a similar prophecy. We have the signs in the heavens in verse 4, focusing more on the stars falling and something new, the heavens rolling up like a scroll.

God doesn't tell us the name of the region that ends up having the ground-seep of oil burning forever, although the land of Edom is part of God's judgment. This kind of terrain fits the Middle East theme well. And the end of the chapter is full of a fascinating list of birds and other creatures who will find a forever home in this once princely region and never be bothered again.

~

Joel 2 could make an epic movie if someone with a big enough imagination took it on. While the near prophecy has to do with a terrible plague of locusts eating everything in sight, you can also think of them as another kind of army we will meet in Revelation. You can read the whole thing if you like, but where things get more clearly focused on still-future events starts in **verse 30**.

We've already looked at the end of the chapter from when Peter quoted it in his Pentecost sermon, but remember how I pointed out that the end doesn't really fit with the first century? And **verse 32** is an important glimpse into what God does with his worshippers when it's time to judge the wicked.

This same flow of events is repeated in **Joel 3:14–16**. Bad guys gather to fight, sun, moon, and stars darken, and God's people find hope.

~

Amos 5:18–20 tells us something interesting about some people who long to see God's day. Amos's people wanted God's protection without obeying his laws. So God compared what it would be like for such people to escaping one wild animal only to be attacked by something even more deadly.

~

Obadiah is a tiny book and it ends with the Day of the Lord and its aftermath. In **verse 15** we are given one of the great KEYS to the end of history. Straight up, God tells us he is purposefully returning bad things onto people who have been horrible to his people. This is an important concept we find all over the place in prophecy.

First, terrible things are done to those who fear God, then he sweeps in with vengeance such as has never been seen and wipes the bad guys out completely. If the evil has not yet been done to us, it is not yet time for God to execute his judgment on the wicked. Period.

The rest of the book gives us a close-up view of how God protects his people and uses them as his warriors to destroy God's enemies.

~

Zephaniah 2:1–3 is part of a larger prophecy that is mostly focused on judgments close at hand, but here it gives us some of the same ideas we've been seeing about the future Day of the Lord.

First Zephaniah tells them to gather together. We don't know if he's telling us they were already going to do this anyway or if this would mean calling a council that could help them make a wise decision. But he then tells them they need to make up their mind before the Day of the Lord starts because... if they will seek God and his meek and righteous ways *they may be hidden away when it's time for his judgment to fall on the wicked.*

~

The last chapter of **Zechariah (14)** is one of the richest future prophecies in the whole Bible. It's got some scary stuff, but includes elements we have seen in other places as well as some clues we are only given here.

- **Verses 1–2**: Israel's enemies are horrible to them; the whole world will be fighting them at once.
- **Verse 4**: Jesus himself will stand on the Mount of Olives just east of Jerusalem, and it splits.

We know there is a fault line that runs through this hill. It will just take a major earthquake to finish what we can see is waiting to happen.

Verse 5 tells us a secret about what will happen to some Jewish people at this time. No one knows what this "valley reaching to Azal" is, but it's going to open a way of escape for the Jewish people. Then Jesus himself will show up with his "saints." We're going to be seeing a lot more of these "holy ones" as we move into the New Testament.

All the things we've seen about the Day of the Lord get moved into one verse for Zechariah in **14:6**. It is a "unique" day and the one thing we find out about it here is that it will be neither light nor dark. Unlike many prophecies, this one has to be only a single day, and reading the rest of the chapter walks us through the aftermath of this event:

- First, we have the water flowing from Jerusalem.
- Then we have God establishing his earthly reign as king of the whole world.
- Then we have even more rearrangement of the elevation of Jerusalem and its area.

And finally, we circle around to what happened to wipe out the bad guys starting in **verse 12**. **Verse 13** mentions how God is going to turn armies against each other so they start to wipe the others out. But that's not nearly as exciting as what God himself does to the rest. This you might have seen in a movie. You'll want to remember how all their soft tissues turn to soup, and **verse 15** tells us it's not just the men, but their animals get melted down to muck too. We're going to see more of this bloody goop in Revelation.

Verse 16 starts one of the most extraordinary passages about the experience of those kingdoms Daniel was told (in Daniel 7:12) would still continue to exist for a time after the Son of Man was given his kingdom. And it gives us a glimpse of just how stern a ruler Jesus is going to be.

If any country doesn't officially go up to Jerusalem to worship God, they won't get rain all year. You might think that sounds amazing, but ask a farmer what they think about having zero rain for a year.

And in Jerusalem, everything, even the decorations on the horses and the cooking pots, will be holy to God. Not having Canaanites doesn't mean God refuses to allow people with rotten parents into his kingdom. Jesus himself gave the Canaanite mom a hard time in Matthew 15:22–29 until she humbled herself under him as an individual.

There are people groups who have refused to worship God for millennia. If I'm one of these people, I can change, but I would no longer be counted as part of the group of "Canaanites."

New Testament

If you know anything about "the Rapture" you'll know a lot about

1 Thessalonians 4

Now it's time for us to turn there and see what Paul has to say!

Verse 13 starts the section. What was Paul's main goal in writing about this? The people around these Christians believed once your body died that was it. No resurrection, you just stop. Forever. A few figured your soul could continue on as a sort of ghost, but only the Jews still believed in the resurrection of the body (Job 19:26; Matthew 11:24).

Verse 14 tells us our loved ones rising is as sure as Jesus's own body coming back to life. When it's time, God will bring those who died with him along with Jesus himself.

Verse 15 assures us that all those who belong to Jesus and die will rise before those who are still alive when it's time for Jesus's coming. That word for "precede" can also mean the living won't be more "important" than those who died. Remember Jesus's teaching on the first shall be last and the last first (Matthew 19:30)? It's not going to matter whether we were born early in history or right at the time Jesus takes over, God loves and honors us all.

Verse 15 gives us another KEY to prophecy. It's not as much teaching us something new as showing us we can't disconnect this passage from others. Paul tells us he and those he is writing with know what comes next because of "the word of the Lord." Do you know who the "Lord" is? Every single time Paul uses it from the first moment Paul meets him in Acts 9:5 he calls *Jesus* his Lord. Other New Testament writers may use "Lord" for all three persons of the Trinity, or the Father alone, but if it's Paul, it is Jesus he is calling Lord.

So, this means Jesus himself talked about what Paul is now telling us. And it's time to see how well this fits with what Jesus did say in the Gospels.

Do you remember the first passage we studied from Jesus? **Verses 16–17** tell us the main markers of what happens when it's time for the dead to rise. How many of these things match what Jesus told us in Matthew 24:30–31? I found six things that totally line up:

- Jesus descending, the trumpet, the clouds, the air, an angel, the gathering of Jesus's people.

And see how there are people who are alive and "remain"? This word isn't a fun one. It means they are *survivors*. Things will not be comfy for them up to that point; they just managed to not get killed somehow.

Let's keep going!

First Paul reminds us this is a great comfort knowing we will be reunited with our loved ones, then he moves on to a wider picture of the end of history. **1 Thessalonians 5** opens a lot like Jesus talking about "seasons" and Paul expects his reader to have a lot of knowledge about what to watch for.

Verses 2–4 need to be read as a set, or people get strange ideas about the Christian experience here. Yes, Jesus will come like a thief; remember he said so himself. But *who* will be shocked? The people saying "peace" and "safety." Are these Jesus's people? No, it's the ones who will experience sudden destruction. Paul tells us we Christians will not be overtaken by "that day."

We've been seeing a lot of that Day, haven't we?

Verse 5 could be our slogan as Jesus's followers. If you are alive at the time all these things happen I have the feeling it will be very precious to you. We are not of the darkness but walk in Jesus's light. We know what's coming; we are alert and watch!

It's sort of surprising to have a list of the kind of spiritual armor Paul wants us to wear in **verse 8**. But when you think about it, facing hard times makes most of us think of moving to the wilderness and stockpiling guns, ammo, and food. Instead, Paul reminds us to keep our faith (Luke 18:8), love (Matthew 24:12), and hope (Luke 21:28) glued on our hearts.

A second KEY to the future comes in **verse 9**. We've already seen how this works, but here Paul tells it to us straight out. We will face plenty of hard times, but never from God. When it's time for him to avenge us, we will be saved by Jesus!

And finally, this whole section has still been part of the thinking Paul expects us to use to comfort each other. **Verse 11** could be read side by side with its sister passage in **Titus 2:13**. It's pointing to the same relief we feel when we remember God's got even scary times like this.

~

Yes, **John 5:25–29** and the next passage are earlier in the Bible, but they make way more sense when you already understand 1 Thessalonians 4.

Here, Jesus is dealing with the Jewish leaders who refuse to see that he is their Messiah and God in human form. He's making the case for him being the judge of humanity. So, he does a kind of reverse "once upon a time" and tells us someday the dead are going to hear his call. Those who are good will have the "resurrection of life" and those who are evil will have a "resurrection of evil."

Daniel told us the same thing; now we know it's Jesus's voice that activates their new life. Neither of these prophecies shows us if any time happens between the good people coming alive and the evil, but that doesn't mean they have to happen back to back.

~

1 Corinthians 15 is one of my favorite passages in the Bible. If you read the full chapter you will get a college-level course in how to build a powerful logic-based argument for what you believe. No one was better at this than Paul, and the topic of the resurrection fired him up.

Like with the people at Corinth, Paul was having to deal with people who had been told no one ever had a second life, after dying you were toast. **Verse 12** opens the section, but for our study of the End Times, things pick up in **verse 23**. Right away he tells us the same thing Jesus already did: Christians will be brought back to life at Jesus's return.

The next few verses give us two KEYS not only for the future but for understanding everything.

Verses 28 is so special that if you make any marks in your Bible at all, this is easily as important a verse as John 3:16 and Psalm 23. But the concept starts in **verse 24**. Jesus is going to become king of the world. Every authority structure on earth is going to be forced to submit to Jesus one way or another.

Finally, **verse 26** tells us the only enemy left will be death itself. This concept is huge for the biblical worldview. Did you know the secular evolutionary view teaches the opposite? Without billions of years of death, they don't have a story for how things could have developed. They have to believe death is a force for good. God tells us it is the final enemy.

Then Paul makes the case for Jesus himself coming under his Father's authority. Everything in history points to the Father, who works through Jesus.

Paul's argument moves back to the here-and-now at this point until **verse 35**. Then things get really interesting, because we all want to know the answer to the question he asks. **Verses 36–38** compare our new bodies to how different a plant is from the seed it grew from. Every seed on earth is so different from the full plant, you would never figure out how it would be transformed with just your imagination.

Verses 42–50 tell us our current bodies—made from Adam's genetics that get damaged, old, and decay when we die—are in a whole different class from the new body Jesus will give us.

Finally in **Verses 51–53** we get the "mystery" of what happens when Jesus comes for us. Not every Christian will die. Some of us will have survived, but all of us will be changed. It won't take more than a split second, and it will happen right when the "last trumpet" sounds. Just like "first" doesn't only mean earliest, calling it the "last" doesn't mean no trumpet is ever allowed to blow after we are changed, but it both marks the Time of the End and it will be the last one that matters for us.

And, like Paul told the Thessalonians, the raising of the dead and the transformation of those still alive happen back to back. Right when the trumpet sounds the call to gather us to Jesus.

Go ahead and read to the end of the chapter. Paul tells us we must be changed from our bodies that can die to those that last forever. He sings Hosea 13:14 about how death can't scare us anymore and rejoices in Jesus's victory over death forever. And then the chapter ends with how we find the strength to serve Jesus and live a life stuffed with good deeds because we remember these things.

~

You'd think that what Paul told this church in his first letter would have been enough for them, but it was only the beginning. Some of the clearest teachings about the timing of The End are found in **2 Thessalonians**, the shortest letter Paul wrote to a church.

We're going to start right near the beginning because it discusses going through difficulties and what God does about it. Go ahead and read the polite opening and then see how his first topic picks up in **verse 4**. These people were going through a hard time. And that word for "hard time"? Yes, it's the same one Jesus used. And here's what really interesting: read down really quickly and you'll see the same word again in verse 6, only it's God who is squeezing people.

Now, we'll go back and read what's going on more carefully. First, the church people are going through persecution, then we have the same KEY concept Obadiah gave us.

Take your time to digest **verses 5–6**. *It is right for God to oppress the bad guys who treat his people like garbage.* He will make sure we are honored and the only way anyone ever escaped his judgment is to hide with him. He also doesn't smash people who *would be* bad guys if they stayed alive long enough. God didn't make baby Adolf Hitler die of a childhood disease, even knowing what he would become.

And have a look at **verse 7**. Have we seen this idea before? Oh, yes. Jesus told it to us and so did Paul in his first letter to the Thessalonians. God's people who have been 'tribulated' (this is the verb made from the word "tribulation") get to rest "with us." And when do these once oppressed people get to rest? When Jesus is revealed with his angels.

But Jesus doesn't just head back to heaven to have a pool party, he's got work to do. The next three verses walk through what he's up to after giving his people a break. First, it's time for Jesus's heavenly flamethrower on those who will not obey God. These aren't people who don't understand; they know perfectly well God is real and should be honored and obeyed. They just won't.

And we get a sense of what eternal destruction looks like. These people will be sent far away from his glory and from everyone honoring God.

Paul doesn't want to stay gloomy though, he pulls us back in **verse 10** to what those of us who love God will be doing. He will be glorified "in" us. (Or "by" us, or "with" us—ask a Greek scholar what this preposition means. God probably means all these things and more.) Not only will we be telling God how amazing he is, he'll be showing the world how amazing he is by what he does with us. And I know I'll be one of those marveling at what God does at this point!

The close of chapter 1 shows us how practical it is to be aware that Jesus is really coming back. If I am constantly remembering Jesus is going to reward and judge everyone based on their faith and obedience today, will I be living for things the world and my flesh tempt me to choose?

Next, we have one of the clearest passages laying out the sequence of End Time events outside of Jesus's prophecy. **Chapter 2** goes right back to the topic of Jesus's return and our being gathered to him. You can see in **verse 2** that the Thessalonian church had somehow gotten the idea that they were already going through the Day of the Lord—the time when Jesus avenges himself on the bad guys. That would be a scary thought!

Paul comforts the church by reminding them two things have to happen before it's time for God's judgment. First, there will be a capital letter Apostasy. While Greek scholars can argue a little about what this word means since the basic meaning is to "fall away," the typical use for this word was the same as our English word. It means a bunch of people will no longer claim to belong to God the way they once did.

Second the "Man of Sin" or "Lawlessness" has to be revealed. It's not enough for him to be alive and working in secret. Before Jesus starts his campaign of destruction against him, this lawless one has to show the whole world he is obviously against God.

In **verse 4** we see this bad dude straight up opposing God himself. In fact, this verse is the clearest in the whole Bible as to how bold this character is. The Abomination of Desolation won't just be a statue, it will be the man himself, sitting there in God's temple, claiming to be god. Woah.

Verses 6–7 are rather frustrating for everybody. Why did Paul and those first Christians get to know who was holding this bad guy back but we don't?

There are a couple of main guesses, but the people who choose one option don't find the case too strong for the other one.

Some people really want it to be the Holy Spirit, but that's mostly people who think all the Christians will have been raptured out of the way before the Man of Sin shows up. But just because that logic is flawed doesn't mean it can't be the Holy Spirit. At the same time there are zero verses that clearly talk about the Holy Spirit restraining anyone like this character does.

Another idea is that this might be Michael the archangel. They use the first verse of Daniel 12 and how Michael "stands up" as evidence for their idea. But the Hebrew word means to 'stand your ground' not 'get out of the way.'

So, anyone who is sure they know exactly what Paul means here is taking the Bible farther than we can really take it. We can go ahead and guess, just not tell everyone they have to believe the same guess too.

Verse 8 skips right from the Man of Sin looming large to what Jesus does to him. And it's really hard to see what's happening just from the English. Jesus will eat him up with his breath the way fire does and "destroy" him with how bright Jesus's coming is. Most translations take this to mean the Man of Sin getting killed here, but it's a lot more complicated than that.

We're going to see how much "fire" is part of Jesus's judgment on the wicked soon. And that word for destroy? It's the same word Paul uses for what happens to our "body of sin" when we become Christians in Romans 6:6. And earlier he uses it for making something "void," "without effect," or even "put out of business" (Romans 3:3, 31, etc.). This word doesn't mean to kill as much as it means to stop it from doing anything powerful.

Could Paul mean "kill" here in 2 Thessalonians? If we didn't have other verses to compare it with, this translation could work, but we know this Man of Sin *never does get killed* by Jesus, instead he is thrown alive into the Lake of Fire (Revelation 19:20). And we already learned he won't be allowed to continue hurting Jesus's people when Jesus shows up in his glory even though this happens some time before he gets tossed off the earth. This is a verse that needs the principle of the two or three witnesses to make sense.

Verses 9–12 wrap up with a frustrating reminder of how much people who don't worship Jesus want to believe lies. All you need to do is listen to the news to see how true this already is. And one of the saddest things to realize is that, at some point, a person or whole group can love their lies so much God makes sure they deeply believe it—so much so that even when horrible things begin to happen because of God's judgment they still won't turn away from them.

Remember Pharaoh who wouldn't let God's people go even when his country had been utterly ruined? Same principle.

~

2 Peter 3 is the last section of writing we have from Peter just before he was crucified for his testimony of Jesus. First, he reminds us to remember both the Old and New Testament writings—he would approve of our study today!

Then he points out that people are going to pretend the Bible can't be trusted to tell the truth about our past or our future. Did you know the same kind of person who doesn't think Jesus is really going to come back and judge sin also doesn't think he did it in the past?

Verses 5–6 tell us something important about how God created the world. First, he used his word to make it, not the natural processes atheistic scientists today claim. And see how the original dry land was made to stand up in and around water? The way the land was held above the ocean was different, and that difference is what made a single worldwide flood possible destroying everything. That's why there will never be another flood like it again.

Next time, Peter tells us in **verse 7**, God is going to use fire instead when he destroys the bad guys.

You are going to hear people use **verse 8**, of all things, when they are like the scoffers from the beginning of the chapter. Lovely Christian people will use God treating millennia as single days to claim God used billions of years to create everything. If you've been paying attention, you know this is not something they actually got from Peter.

Do you remember when you were little and couldn't wait for your birthday to come? Hearing that it was going to take a month was almost unbearable. But you've probably gotten to where a month is easier to wait. Now, this 'shrinking' of time doesn't slow down. If you ask an elderly person what time feels like to them, they would probably say the past decade has passed faster than a year used to when they were young.

God is older than the hills. He likes time—he invented it, but he doesn't experience it the way young whipper-snappers like us do. He is *patient* and *longsuffering*.

The point of this verse is, there is a good reason God hasn't burnt up the bad guys yet, and that's because he doesn't mind waiting. **Verse 9** tells us what's going on. God doesn't want to lose anyone who might possibly reject sin and turn to him instead.

We've seen the idea in **verse 10** before. Do you think Peter was paying attention when Jesus taught his disciples about him coming like a thief? Looks like it! And he mentions this secret coming as he's thinking about the scoffers who are going to be judged.

Here's another KEY to the end times. Lots of people don't even think it's worth the trouble trying to understand this future-focused part of the Bible. And you can see how gigantic a puzzle it is! But **verse 11** could not be clearer. When we remember everything around us is going to end up fried to a crisp, we live differently today.

In fact, if you finish this study and still care more about your video games and the stuff in your closet than you do about loving people and honoring God, I've totally failed. And so did Jesus, Daniel, Paul, Peter, and John. But like Peter, I'm sure you'll read the last few verses he gave us, his beloved lambs (John 21:15). We are being invited to live clean lives, treating the Bible right, not getting tricked like the wicked, and growing in Jesus's grace!

~

We already talked about how John both told us the Antichrist was coming and lots of antichrists were already around. Now I want you to notice what they do.

1 John 2:18 tells us John and his readers are already in the "last times" because the same kinds of characters are already on the scene. And, of course, he is right. Ever since the New Testament was first written, people have believed Jesus could come back very soon. This is what Peter meant by telling us days and millennia are interchangeable for God. In his experience, it's only felt like two days since Jesus went back to heaven.

Verse 19 tells us a lot more about what Paul told the Thessalonians about the "falling away." These people who are opposed to Jesus were once part of the church, but they don't stay.

Then, like Daniel 12:10 told us, John points out that God's people understand something the wicked can't. And the main truth we know is in **verses 22–23**: Jesus is God and he became a real human with a body just like ours. This is something those who fall for the Antichrist's lies refuse to believe.

Go ahead and keep reading through the end of the chapter because **verse 28** tells us that understanding these realities is what will help us be bold and brave when it's time to meet Jesus at his return. Because he IS coming.

And **1 John 3:2** tells us something extra special. When Jesus shows up, he's going to make us like him. Something about seeing him is going to transform us to match him. And the next verse reminds us that knowing this inspires us to live a Jesus-style life of purity (Verse 5 reminds us we can only do this if we are living in Jesus; we sure can't pull it off in our own power.)

~

The one other place the Bible calls the bad guy "Antichrist" is in **2 John 1:7–8**. We don't really learn anything new, but John tells us again that what marks someone opposed to Jesus is that they lie about him ever becoming human. The other reason John warns us of these evil people is so we can receive our full reward. It makes me wonder if some of Jesus's people will sort of believe the Lie and end up with less to show for their lives when he comes back.

~

Jude is a tiny book written by one of Jesus's half-brothers, and most of it is focused on watching out for messed-up people in the church. Right in the middle, Jude throws in a quote from one of the most ancient people in history. We aren't told how he knows this, but in **verse 14** he tells us Enoch gave us a prophecy about the end times—and he lived before Noah!

Enoch predicted that God was going to come to earth himself with a bunch of his holy ones. And what does he do then? Deal with the bad guys who do evil things and say evil things against God. Wow, you would think this ancient prophet knew the same things all these other prophets were telling us.

You can keep reading about the kinds of things the wicked people do and what we as Jesus's followers should do. **Verses 22–23** give us good advice both for every day and especially as we see the end coming close. We can be gentle with people who are having a hard time believing the truth but always remember where sin will lead them. You do not want to stay on God's bad side; there is only fire for those who refuse to let go of their sin.

The last two verses of Jude are some of the most special to all Christians but will be particularly precious to those facing the Great Persecution just before Jesus comes to rescue us. He can, and will, help us stand the test if we ask him to. And we will live in his presence one day.

Revelation

Well, we finally got there! Took long enough, but you see how much God had already told us before giving us a whole book about the future.

And if you've skipped ahead to this point, stop. Go back and read the book from the beginning. 'Cause Jesus and John assume you have read the rest of the Bible before you get to the last book. In fact, John quotes the Old Testament over 500 times. The whole book won't make much sense if you read it out of that giant context.

Right away in **verse 1**, we find out these events have to happen "soon." What? Does this mean this prophecy had to happen over 1900 years ago? Here's another way to put the phrase: "what has to happen very quickly." Could it have happened soon after John finished writing? Sure. John, Jude, and the author of Hebrews (1:2) all said it was the last days in the first century, just as Moses had predicted in **Deuteronomy 31:29**. But did everything in the book of Revelation have to happen within the first hundred years after Jesus went to heaven? Not based on the actual words of the Bible.

The Old Testament gives us more clues about this idea of "soon" or "quickly." **Haggai 2:6** tells us God is going to shake the world "in a little while." But do you know when this prophecy of Jesus's coming was made? Haggai was inspiring the Jewish people to rebuild the temple after its destruction 500 years before Jesus came to earth. God's idea of "quickly" and "at hand" is not the same as ours.

Verse 3 tells us something extraordinary about reading and studying this book. I'm sure Jesus knew how many of his people would find his revelation both scary and confusing. So, while places like Psalm 119 and Luke 11:28 tell us we can be blessed by reading the whole Bible, this is the only book to tell us we get a special blessing for being willing to tackle it. Just be sure to do more than read it. There are things for us to obey and remember here, and you will be held responsible for what you now understand.

We're going to see how much John and Jesus like to remind us of God's true character. And the older you get, the more you will discover fear and temptation grow best when we forget who God really is. **Verse 4** tells us God has always been and always will be. How else could he lay out the future for us unless he is there? **Isaiah 46:9–10** tells us this ability is part of what makes him the true God.

Why seven spirits? We're going to run into a lot of symbolic things in this book and we know seven is one of God's favorite numbers. Whether it's the seven days of the week (Exodus 20:11) or wisdom's seven pillars (Proverbs 9:1), God uses it to show completeness.

The list of accomplishments for Jesus in **verse 5** is wide ranging. I remember being puzzled by his being the "firstborn" from the dead. But that was before I understood that Jesus is the first person to die but never face death again. Everyone else who was raised from the dead went on to live ordinary lives, died, and that time stayed dead. Jesus is the first one to truly conquer death and, with his blood, create antibodies against it for us to share.

Have you thought about what **verse 6** teaches before? This book will help you escape the silly idea that God's people spend eternity floating around on fuzzy clouds with only a harp for company. Jesus is directly under the Father, but we are next under him as both religious leaders and governmental rulers.

We've seen a lot of what John tells us in **verse 7**. If you still have any thinking that Jesus is going to sneak around in secret, just read this verse again. The Earth Dwellers are not going to be happy when every one of them sees him.

And why does it mention those who pierced Jesus being part of this group? This book wasn't even written until around 60 years after Jesus's crucifixion, so even if it happened that year very few, if any, of the people who were in power at that time were still alive. One way to make sense of this is to realize the demons in charge of the evil people of the Sanhedrin will still be around when Jesus returns. Or it could be the same class of people since the Pharisees have disciples living to this day.

If you were a student of Greek in John's day, you didn't study the same alphabet we use; theirs started with *alpha* and finished up with *omega*. *Zeta* was near the beginning, not at the end. So, calling Jesus the A and Ω in **verse 8** is saying he is the one at the beginning and still there at the close as well as everywhere in the middle too. And just in case we forgot already, this is talking about time. Oh, BTW, God is not limited in power except by his character. Never by him being too weak or small to pull it off.

Remember that horrible time Jesus predicted is coming when the Abomination of Desolation appears in Jerusalem? The same word for persecution or tribulation is right here in **verse 9**, and John tells us he is our companion as we all go through the universal hard times of Jesus's people. In his case, he'd been stuck on an island because he wouldn't stop talking about Jesus.

Early church records tell us the Romans had already tried to murder John at this point by dipping him in boiling oil, but he wouldn't die. So rather than try some other horrific way to kill him, they just dumped him on a little island in the Aegean Sea not too far from Asia Minor. His letter didn't have that far to travel to those seven churches.

John couldn't get to a healthy local church to worship with on the Lord's Day (the first day of the week that we call Sunday), instead, God sends him a vision. First, he hears a voice. Jesus's resurrection (and pre-human) voice is hard for people to describe, sometimes it sounds like a massive waterfall (verse 15), but at the moment it sounds like—tah-ran-ta-ra!—a trumpet.

We've already talked about everything Jesus says at first and we'll get to the churches one by one soon, so read down to **verses 13–15**. Interestingly, Jesus here looks exactly like the Ancient of Days who gives the Son of Man authority to rule in Daniel 7:9. The only extra details we get about Jesus here are that his eyes are glowing hot, he's got a gold sash, and the fiery stuff is part of his feet rather than flowing around him.

If I saw someone whose face was as bright as the sun, I would fall on my face too. It would be the one chance my eyes, and probably my life, had of surviving!

Let's pause to think about Jesus's robe for a minute. John doesn't tell us it's white here, but other places mention the color. Mark 9:3 tells us Jesus's clothes turned dazzlingly white while he talked with Moses and Elijah. God's clothes are described as brilliant light in Psalm 104:1–2. In Matthew 28:2–4, an angel's white clothing is part of what terrifies the guards at Jesus's tomb. Here in Revelation we'll see more characters, including millions of humans, all wearing the same white clothing.

We'll see more about how we get such clean clothes later, but it's worth taking time to notice that, from the least in the kingdom to God himself, everyone wears the same "uniform." Jesus, the greatest of all, only gets a gold sash to mark his rank. That's nothing like the difference between the underclass and the monarch of any earthly kingdom.

Verse 18 tells us something we could guess at, but now we know for sure. We already knew Jesus couldn't be hurt by death ever again, now we find out he'd won for himself the keys to both death and hell. Oh, yes, we'll see more of this near the end of the book, but did you know Satan has never yet visited hell and he wants nothing to do with it? Jesus is the ruler of everything, even of the place of torment for those who reject him.

And speaking of keys, **verse 19** gives us a KEY for understanding this whole book. Some of what he's writing was true already and happening as Jesus talked to John, but some of it wouldn't happen until later. Easy, yes, but some important Bible scholars have gotten tripped up by not understanding this.

I didn't try to explain the lampstands and stars earlier because I knew Jesus would tell us in **verse 20**. Pretty much any object John sees in this book, even when it's real, is a symbol for something spiritual.

Revelation 2-3

The next two chapters are important ones for our Christian life in general, but the events Jesus discusses in them happened long ago. Many prophecy teachers assume these mini letters to churches in a circuit around Asia Minor must be prophecy too since the rest of the book is. My question for them is, does the Bible tell us this? Did Jesus say he was talking about the future here? Or did they add this idea on their own?

We can have ideas and test them against what the Bible says, but when we have ideas and change how we read the Bible because of our ideas, this is a big problem. At some point, where do you stop? Every "Christian" group on earth tries to get the Bible to agree with them, even when what they believe is 180 degrees from what God actually meant.

If you look up a map of where these churches were based, you'll see the order takes you from the starting church near the coast and slopes around to form a chain. Each letter is presented in the order a mail carrier would have delivered them.

Plus, there's this problem: every teacher who uses these churches as eras thinks we are in the last one, the Church of Laodicea. It was a wealthy church who needed to let Jesus provide for them what they really needed. Try telling the Christians in sub-Saharan Africa or the restricted countries of Asia that they are really too full of their own wealth to crave Jesus's and see how they take it!

Even though this section is about the different conditions of any church at any time, there are a couple of things that fit into our study. Go ahead and read these chapters for yourself and I'll skip to the points that matter for the future.

Verses 4–5 give us the problems Jesus has with this otherwise great church. It's interesting that Jesus had warned us the love of many would grow cold in Matthew 24:12. Does this church give us a glimpse into one of the ways this happens? Then I want you to notice that this mostly amazing church is the only one of the seven that gets threatened with the removal of its candlestick. Like Paul told us in 1 Corinthians 13, Jesus seriously requires us to have love.

Every church section closes with a statement about listening to the Holy Spirit and the reward promised to the "overcomers." Jesus may be the one who gave the message to John, but the Spirit is just as involved in communicating truth, only behind the scenes (2 Peter 1:21). An overcomer is anyone who makes it through all the obstacles to arrive safely in God's kingdom. Don't you worry, if you belong to Jesus, he will help you get there (John 6:37–39). Only those who try to earn God's favor in their own strength will fail (Matthew 7:21–23).

Here are the seven things promised us:

- 2:7 We will eat of the Tree of Life in the middle of God's "paradise" (garden)

This tree once stood in Eden, now it's in God's new kingdom.

- 2:11 We won't be hurt by the 2nd Death
- 2:17 We will eat the "hidden manna," and each of us will get a white stone with a secret name only Jesus and you know

When Moses was done having the Ark of the Covenant built, he was told to put a pot of manna inside to remind the people of how God had fed them all those years (Exodus 16:33). No one was to mess with it, but we will get fed by this same food someday. The white stone could be connected with ancient customs of using a stone to represent a person, but the Bible doesn't really give us any direct clues.

- 2:26 – 28 We will receive power over the nations to rule and smash them with an "iron rod," and we get the "Morning Star"
- 3:5 We get a white garment to wear, our name left in the Book of Life (more in chapter 20), and Jesus will announce his connection with us in front of the Father and his angels
- 3:12 We will become a "pillar" in God's temple without having to leave, and God will have his own, his city's, and Jesus's new name written on us

If you're anything like me, being told you'll be a pillar that can't ever leave the temple sounds more like a terrible curse than a reward. But Galatians 2:9 tells us the leaders of the church were "pillars." Peter didn't get turned into a real rock back then! And eventually God's temple is going to be *everywhere* (Revelation 21:22), so being 'stuck' in it just means you won't be visiting the Lake of Fire.

- 3:21 We get to sit on Jesus's throne with him

That's a pretty serious list of rewards for those who make it to Jesus's kingdom!

Just a few more verses come up when studying the future in this section. **Revelation 2:22** mentions that those who mess around with the fake prophetess will be thrown into "great tribulation" or trouble. Yes, it is the same phrase Jesus used in Matthew 24:21. It's also the same phrase Stephen uses in **Acts 7:11** to describe the terrible time the eleven sons of Jacob had that forced them to buy food in Egypt. It just means these people were, or will be, in serious trouble.

Revelation 3:3 warns a church to repent or Jesus will come on them like a thief. What? I thought Paul told us we didn't need to worry about this. But remember, Jesus points out that at this Sardis church almost everyone there is dead. They don't really belong to him except in name, so they won't have the bad guys giving them a hard time like the real Christians. We already see this today when churches go along with the world's ideas about morality, politics, and false thinking of all kinds. Even the atheists like them! But it's not going to be pretty for such people when Jesus comes.

Revelation 3:10 is a favorite for those who want to place Jesus's gathering of his people at the very beginning of End Time events. It sounds good if you don't know any better. First, we already know we aren't going to have to face the time when the world has its big trial. But more than this, the phrase "keep from" is also in Jesus's prayer in **John 17:15**. Read it and tell me whether Jesus meant that he expected his people to vanish up into heaven there.

Anyone who uses Revelation 3:10 to prove the Rapture happens at the beginning of End Time events has not been careful with their interpretation.

Revelation 3:18 isn't explaining the future, but I figure you might find what Jesus says kind of crazy. He first tells them they are so poor they don't even have clothes and then tells them to "buy" gold, clothes, and eye medicine from him. How is this supposed to work? **Isaiah 55:1** gives us the same idea. God tells his people to buy food from him "without price." He uses this idea of buying to show how salvation is something we get from him but we cannot earn. I'm surprised Jesus didn't tell them, "Just say please."

Revelation 4

Now it's going to get way more interesting! John hears a voice calling him up through a door into heaven. We don't have this distinction in English, but, like a number of languages, Greek had a command for one person and a different form for more than one. The command to "come" is in the single-person form. It cannot mean a whole slew of people being "raptured."

It is also common for pastors and even scholars to point out something that's missing here. From Revelation 4 on, until a single mention in Revelation 22:16, we don't find the word "church" in the whole book. Teachers will tell us this means the "church" isn't there because they've been raptured. But this is a problem on a couple of levels.

First, it is a logical fallacy to claim that because God didn't use a particular *word* he didn't mean a particular *idea*. Unitarians use this logic to deny that God is a trinity since the word "trinity" doesn't occur anywhere in the whole Bible. Some people deny there will be a rapture at all because the Bible never uses the word "rapture." But both these concepts are clearly there in the Bible *using other terms*. And so are the people who might be called the "church."

For example, the same people who claim the church must be gone from earth because the word isn't in the book of Revelation don't claim the book of Romans isn't for the church because the word only shows up in the last chapter. And the entire book of 1 John—written by the same author as Revelation—doesn't use the word church. Does this mean nothing in these passages is for people who are part of the church? No one has ever claimed this. But they use this same logic to defend their traditional belief about the Rapture.

Secondly, John is being taken off the earth and up to heaven in chapter 4. If we can assume these people are NOT there any time their name is not used, then the church cannot be raptured at this point since they were still on earth in chapter 3 and no change is ever mentioned about the church after that. The church also wouldn't get to come back to earth with Jesus in chapter 19 or even show up in the Eternal State in chapters 21–22. Not a single person believes this because it is nonsense. What they don't realize is their own belief that the church got raptured because Jesus and John stop talking about the "church" is just as big a fallacy.

Some scholars will even use the phrase "after this" to mean "after the church is raptured." They reason that because John is done sending letters to the individual churches and switches to his vision, the whole church has to be out of the picture. Let's see how this works if we use the same logic for the rest of John's writings. The first time he uses "after this" is in John 3:22 when Jesus and the disciples move on from Nicodemus's night visit. Does this phrase mean Nicodemus must have left the earth before they traveled back to Judea? And in John 21:1 did the disciples have to leave earth before having breakfast with Jesus on the beach?

John uses the exact phrase "after this" eight times in his Gospel and again in Revelation five more times, usually interpreted to simply mean a sequence of events. If he wanted to say, "Jesus tells the churches stuff and after listening to him I heard a voice..." how else could he have said it any clearer?

The kind of Bible interpretation many people use for Revelation 4:1 is totally unlike the way they handle the rest of the Bible. In 2 Timothy 2:14–21, Paul urges Timothy and those under him to be extra careful how they use the Word of God, or else. If you have to use a style that would never work on the rest of the Bible to get it to say what you want it to, are you really honoring God's Word the way he deserves?

So back to what John actually tells us. He is told he's going to see things that happen in the future. What I love is that God brings him up to heaven before any of the events that will transfer the authority over earth. In this chapter, we are seeing the last day of the 'normal' heaven *the way it is happening right now.*

First, we see God's throne. Not surprising, since the Father is the most important being in the universe, of course he draws John's attention. The stones and colors have inspired people for centuries. What we call jasper comes in a rainbow of colors from green to red to gold-flecked white while the carnelian comes in yellows and orange. It's possible God wanted us to picture all these colors.

It's also possible that God wanted us to remember he is the one who invented such beautiful minerals. We have always used precious stones as symbols of how wealthy and powerful a king is, and, since early times, many people have assumed they have magical powers. Today people still buy certain stones if they are feeling stressed or tired. These stones weren't meant to control us; they are under God's control, and he is the most powerful king the universe has ever known.

Verse 4 introduces us to our first heavenly citizens, and they have puzzled us ever since John's book was written. Why 24 dudes? Do we know who they are? 24 is 12 twice, which makes us think of the sons of Jacob and the 12 disciples. But John *was* one of the disciples and we aren't told he had any weird time-travel doppelganger issues! Many people assume these guys aren't even human; after all, angels wear white and look like men too.

These "elders" (which can either mean old or high ranking—like generals) are wearing the standard-issue heavenly clothes: white robes. But they also have gold crowns and thrones, the same name for chairs used to describe God's own. While I am content to leave their exact identity fuzzy, there is nowhere in Scripture that angels are giving the marks of kings, but human beings are (Daniel 7:18, 27; Romans 8:17; 2 Timothy 2:12; Revelation 1:6, 5:10, 20:6, 22:5)

John's attention is quickly brought back to God's throne because in **verse 5** he notices the lightning and rumbling voices coming out of it. Then he spots seven torches that he somehow knows are the seven spirits of God himself.

We're going to see the next element of God's throne room again in a later chapter and find out that it's massive. **Verse 6** tells us there is a "sea of glass." I've always pictured this as something like a huge ice skating rink, as clear as a lake that froze without any snow falling.

But John's attention quickly moves from this unmoving feature to something much more captivating, four "living creatures." What is interesting about the way John describes them is that a prophet had already seen these weird beings. But when Ezekiel (**1:5–13**) saw them, they all had all four characteristics, while here each looks different from the rest. Also, when

Ezekiel saw them, they only had four wings (1:6) while John sees them with six, more like what Isaiah (**6:2**) saw. If these are the same creatures as Isaiah's, then they are called "Seraphim" or "fiery ones."

Ezekiel also saw these creatures with giant wheels that had bunches of eyes (**Ezekiel 1:18**). But it was clear to him that the spirit of the creatures was in the wheels (**Ezekiel 1:20–21**). Perhaps when they aren't being used as a divine transport system they absorb the wheels inside themselves and just have the eyes in their bodies?

Oh look, John's creatures are clearly the same as Isaiah's because they are the only ones to have the same job: proclaiming God's superlative holiness. You studied "superlatives" in English class, right? There are descriptions, then comparisons, then superlatives: good, better, best. And God is the holiest of all possible beings. So, that's what these four creatures spend their time reminding everyone about. Plus, they remind us what we've already seen several times in this book, that God was, is, and will always be. And did we remember he can do anything because he's all-powerful? Oh, yeah.

They must take a break between these announcements because the 24 dudes have time to pick up their crowns in between throwing sessions. But **verse 10** tells us when the creatures call out, the elders take off their crowns, throw them at God's feet and start their own praise session.

And they say the same thing everything in the universe should be telling God. He deserves all the credit and honor and worship because he made the whole shebang—because he felt like it.

Revelation 5

Now it's finally time for us to start tying together the events of the future. Only took John four chapters to get there, and at this point he dives right in.

I've read where people insist this scroll has seven seals all through it, allowing the reader to break one seal and unroll a bit before reaching the next seal. The problem is, there is nothing in history to suggest anyone ever figured out a way to do this, and it's only something you would come up with if the theology you already had *made* you see it this way.

Here's how seals were actually used in the ancient world. Since earliest times, an important person would have a carved ring, stamp, or roller that could be pressed into wax or clay to mark an object as official. Joseph was given Pharaoh's signet ring as a mark of his power (Genesis 41:42), and in the Book of Esther, the king first gives his ring to Haman (Esther 3:10–11) and then to Mordechai (8:10). Each time the seal marked the actions of the person as flowing from the king's power.

These seals were still used all the time in the first century AD, and we even saw the practice of marking something official when the stone was "sealed" by the Pharisees in **Matthew 27:66**, although we have to go to the Old Testament to find the Bible mentioning scrolls being sealed. One of the more interesting ways to see how these seals were used for official documents is in **Isaiah 29:11**. It wasn't that the scholar didn't have the strength to open the scroll, he lacked the authority to break the seal without getting in trouble.

So, now we're in heaven and we get a super-over-the-top official scroll being held by...God the Father himself. We are never directly told what the writing on the scroll represents, so we'll have to watch what happens when the final seal gets broken.

Knowing all this helps us understand why the angel calls for someone "worthy" to open the scroll. We need someone with official authority who won't get in trouble with God for daring to take something so important.

Verses 3–4 set us up for one of the biggest ideas in the universe. Remember how we learned Adam and Eve were made the rulers of the whole world on Day 6 of Creation Week (**Genesis 1:28**)? But right away they submitted to Satan (**Genesis 3**), so sin and death reigned over everyone from that time on (**Romans 5:12–14**). This left us in an impossible trap.

No wonder John weeps. We and the universe were totally sunk.

But then along came Jesus, who sacrificed himself to redeem his kin (**Leviticus 25:47–49**)! This is why John sees him as a violently-slaughtered lamb rather than a roaring lion here. It was his death that paid the price to buy us back, so he appears the way a zombie sheep might—except he's clearly alive and in his right mind, but bearing some major wounds. And his odd extra horns and eyes are explained to us right away. The Holy Spirit is closely tied to Jesus, sharing his power, knowledge, and the ability to act around the globe.

So, when Jesus takes the scroll from the Father in **verse 7**, all three parts of the Godhead are there, working together to complete their plan for earth's history.

Next, we get a clearer picture of the job of both the 24 elders and the living creatures. They see the act of the Lamb, preparing to set in motion the most powerful events in history and they break out in worship. The elders have two things they use besides their voices: harps and incense bowls.

Americans aren't generally into incense much, but it was important to early people and still is in many cultures. God even gave Moses a secret recipe for the kind of incense he liked (Exodus 30:34–38). I own a mite coin from the 2nd Temple period. It's really rough, but you can still see the image of a censor hanging from metal rods. This kind of 'bowl' would allow a priest to swing the smoke of the burning incense back and forth so the widest area could smell the sweet fragrance.

Along with the smell and the harp music, both the elders and creatures sing a song. And it spells out what I just explained about how Jesus was the only person who could win back the kingdom Adam and Eve had forfeited. He redeemed people from all different people groups and put us in charge of both government and worship.

Then suddenly in **verse 11** we finally get more than 32 characters in the greatest throne room of all time. And there is a massive crowd—of angels. It's fun how John tries to give us an estimate of how many there were; the best he can do is say "millions and millions!" And they join in with the praise announcing that Jesus is worthy to receive the power and adoration.

Perhaps one of the most incredible passages in the whole book is the end of this chapter. No matter where a creature is, even if all they are is a fossil (the things under the earth?), even if they never submit to Jesus during their mortal life, every one of us—just by existing—declares Jesus is the one who deserves the eternal praise, honor, glory, and power.

The chapter wraps up with the lead worship team chiming in, *Oh, yes!*

Revelation 6

Been wondering when things will start happening? It's finally time. As Jesus cracks open each seal, one of the living creatures calls John over to see what gets unleashed.

Lots of End Time teachers are sure they know who the being riding the white horse is. They often claim it's the Antichrist—the Lawless One who brings the Abomination of Desolation. Some claim it's Jesus himself, riding a white horse to begin taking over the earth. But let's step back a bit from this first horseman and look at all four together.

Here's the whole set:

- Conquering
- War
- Famine
- Death

If you are going to have Horse Rider #1 be an identifiable human being, you're going to need to do it for the other three. And no one has ever suggested the other three horsemen are identifiable characters. So, for me, while I can see the Antichrist's career progress in the white horse's rider, I also see his destructive path through the other three.

These riders seem to be more general "spirits" of the attitudes and experiences of earth at this point. In fact, this idea lines up with an Old Testament passage. Zechariah had a vision of the same color horses in **Zechariah 6:1–8**. There, the prophet isn't told what the different colors mean, but he is told they are four "winds" or spirits that go out from standing before the Lord of the whole earth. It is pretty clear John was seeing something very similar to what Zechariah saw, but none of these riders are expected to be human beings.

And it's important to notice all of these elements are things happening today. They have been happening since Cain murdered Abel, and, in all of human history, they have never *not* been happening. What changes as Jesus breaks each seal is that they get blown to worldwide proportion.

Now let's zoom back in.

First, the white rider is given a crown in **verse 2**. Because this happens when Jesus opens the first seal, most interpreters assume God gave the crown of authority to the white rider. But this doesn't mean the conqueror is *good*. Jesus told Pontius Pilate he only had his power because God had given it (John 19:11) even though Pilate was the one who sided with Herod and the Jewish leaders to murder Jesus. And Paul tells us straight up that all authority is given by God (Romans 13:1) at a time when the chief authority in Rome was fine with throwing Christians to the lions.

Second comes a red rider who is given the ability to "take away peace" from the earth. It's interesting to think of people as trying to cling to peace and having it stolen away from them. And when peace is taken, people turn to killing each other.

Third comes the rider on the black horse. We don't use old-fashioned balance scales often, but we still use scales at the grocery store all the time to weigh out food. And that's what this dude has the scales to do. He's announcing it will cost a typical laborer a full day's wages to buy one quart/kilogram of wheat or three quarts/kg of barley.

This means it will take a hard day's work to earn money to barely keep one person fed well enough to keep working hard, or three people alive on low-quality food. Nothing would be left over for a home, cooking fuel, medicine, or anything else. This is what the world has always feared: a famine.

At the same time, the black horse guy is told not to hurt the oil or wine. These foods are delicacies for the rich. Whether the areas that grow these products aren't affected or, more likely, the supply of specialty foods is still getting to the wealthy, we don't really know. But my guess would be a lot of the famine comes because of the wars and conquering, perhaps with some natural disaster stuff we aren't told about mixed in. This would make a huge class distinction between the poor people who are being attacked and the rich people living in the conqueror's home territory. All the Bible tells us here for sure is, there is famine for basic foods and plenty of fancy food.

Then comes the fourth horse rider. The color of this one is straight out of a horror story. Some Bibles say it's "pale," others "ashen" or "sickly-looking." It's actually worse than this. It's a kind of weird green color, like the horse had died of some horrible disease. And that's what this horse represents. "Death" is the name of the rider himself and hell is following behind gathering up the souls of those whose bodies were beginning to decay. Ewww.

There are a couple of important things to notice in **verse 8**. First, a full quarter of everyone on earth dies right here. Like with the famine, it is possible that across the globe every household of four people will lose one. But if you talk to your parents, they can tell you about the huge numbers of people who died of things like this rider uses—all while they lived normal lives without really noticing except for watching the news. Throughout history, some parts of the world would see vast loss of life while others were perfectly fine. Again, I can't be sure that's what will happen here, but it fits well with the conquering and war theme.

And, it is clear war is a big part of this huge amount of death. It's important to think through what does all these people in:

- Sword
- Famine
- Plague
- Wild animals

If you ever meet someone who has been through a war, they are going to be all too familiar with these deadly weapons. People die directly from the fighting, bombs, and mines. They also die from the farmers not being able to grow food or transport it to hungry areas (This happened in Europe at the end of World War II even after the fighting had stopped.). Where you have people near each other without proper sanitation (water, toilets, soap, etc.) who aren't eating well, you get terrible epidemics that sweep through the survivors.

The wild animals could represent two different things, and might well end up being both. First, they could actually be, well, wild animals. If you are living in makeshift housing as far from the deadly city as you can, there will be real wild animals. And if you have drought or other natural events causing

65

the land to not grow enough food, you'll have hungry wild animals. There are plenty of places around the world where many people die each year from snakes, wild cats, and all kinds of dangerous creatures.

The other possibility is that these are "wild beasts" the way we saw in Daniel. They could be the nations rising and killing people without it being war. Lots of scholars think the Bible means violent people here. But why not lump such cruelty into the "sword"? Either way, I'm sure there will be dead people from real animals alongside lots of people dead from evil humans.

At this point we have a shift in focus. We'd been watching with the living creatures as events are being sent to earth. With the cracking open of the fifth seal our attention is brought back up to heaven and we are introduced to a new set-piece in the throne room. There's an altar up there. And it's the single most important piece of furniture for us.

The book of Hebrews spends the middle part building a case for Jesus being the greatest priest to ever offer sacrifices to God. And in **Hebrews 9:11–14**, it tells us Jesus offered his own life as a sacrifice in the real tabernacle. Not the shadow copy like Moses had built (Hebrews 8:5), but the real one in heaven. How it works with him being both priest and sacrifice only God knows, but the place he offered himself was at this location John looks at here.

Now we see that the altar where Jesus offered the ultimate sacrifice that cleans us from all sin forever (Hebrews 10:10) has something under it. Or, rather, some*bodies*. There is a bunch of "souls" underneath. John describes them as "martyrs," people who had been murdered because they told everyone they belonged to Jesus.

Verses 10–11 hold a KEY to understanding the timeline of End Time events. Look at how these martyrs feel about God and his actions. Do they think the four horsemen were God's messengers for punishment on the Earth Dwellers? If they did, they would not be yelling their complaints at God for dawdling. They are not happy with how long God is taking to avenge their murders on those who hated them for loving Jesus.

From the first through the fifth seals God is not punishing evil.

If he were, why are so many of his own people getting murdered and are now mad at him for doing nothing? They are in heaven; they know God is real and their witness was for the truth at this point. They just don't know the future yet.

After the souls shout like this, God responds in two ways. First, he has them given white robes. Let's think about this a minute. Do you think these are fully-resurrected people who had been hanging out under the altar stark naked until now?

That doesn't seem like something God would do. Jesus had pleaded with the people of the Laodicean church to ask him for white clothes in Revelation 3:18. **2 Corinthians 5:1–4** talks about how our new bodies will cover us so we won't be naked. Revelation 16:15 warns people not to lose their spiritual clothes or else they will be ashamed. Many times in the Old Testament, having no clothes is described as the most embarrassing thing that could happen to you.

If shaming them doesn't make sense for God to do to his extra special witnesses, then why are they only now getting clothes? How about this: Jesus hasn't given the call for the big resurrection yet. Remember how Jesus will call out and the dead will rise (John 5:25–29)? And he does this only after the sun, moon, and stars are darkened (Matthew 24:29–31)? These "souls" are just that, souls of people whose mortal bodies died and they hadn't been given immortal bodies yet (1 Corinthians 15:53–54).

Just as important is the news God gives them. They are asked to wait only a little longer until the full number of their group has been murdered.

Way back in Genesis God introduced this concept. A people group is assigned a "cup of iniquity" and it is only when it is full of sin that God brings ultimate judgment. God told Abraham this was why he wasn't giving the land to him yet.

- In **Genesis 15:16** God told Abraham it would take four generations for the Amorites to fill their cup so they deserved to be destroyed.
- Jesus told the Pharisees they were filling up their fathers' cup to bring judgment on their heads for the murder of every prophet in **Matthew 23:32–35**.
- We will see this again in **Revelation 18:6**

Remember how 2 Thessalonians 1 told us God is righteous to return tribulation on those who tribulate us? That's what we see here. God has set for himself a certain number of martyrs he will endure. But the moment that last Christian is murdered, it's time. And we're about to see just how short a time they had to wait for the last death to clear the way for judgment!

The Pivot Point of History

Verse 12 swings the main players on earth around so fast everyone ends up with whiplash. Jesus cracks open the sixth seal and suddenly we go from magnified but common events to phenomena so extraordinary everyone knows it's God who is doing them.

Six things happen that cause people to react:

- A great earthquake
- The sun is darkened
- The moon turns deep red
- The stars fall
- Heaven is rolled up like a scroll
- All mountains and islands (mountains sticking out of the ocean) are moved

We're going to see a lot more earthquakes coming up, but even this first one is a doozy. It's so massive every high place on the planet is affected. And not only is the earth itself unstable, but everything in outer space gets seriously messed up. We've seen the sun dark before in prophecy, here John describes it as turning black "like sackcloth." In places like Israel, they keep black goats and use their hair to make a rough, scratchy cloth that works great for tents and—sacks.

Some people want all these events in the sky to be natural ones. And it makes sense at first. Meteor showers happen all the time. In 1833 AD a shower with as many as 100,000 meteors an hour appeared over the southern United States. A lot of people at the time thought they were seeing Revelation 6:13

happen right then and there! But they didn't pay attention to the other five signs, did they?

Some people want all the events in the sky to be natural ones. And it makes sense at first. Meteor showers happen all the time. In 1833 AD a shower with as many as 100,000 meteors an hour appeared over the southern United States. A lot of people at the time thought they were seeing Revelation 6:13 happen right then and there! But they didn't pay attention to the other five signs, did they?

If you've ever seen a lunar eclipse you've seen the moon turn red. So this is easy to picture as a natural event—in one location, for a little while. Well, except for this: how do you make the sun dark at the same time you can still see the moon? If you've seen a solar eclipse you know the moon is not shining at the same time. The moon has its dark side to earth and only shows up as it blocks the sun's rays for a few minutes. And the area that can see the sun darkened is only 50 miles wide.

I've also seen the moon turn a similar rusty color when there was a bunch of ash in the upper atmosphere after forest fires in the American West, so some people say all these events are just in earth's atmosphere and not out in space. But if you had something in the atmosphere so think it made the sun look like black cloth, you would not still be seeing the moon.

Then there is the sign of the heavens moving away like a scroll being rolled up. This is almost word for word like Isaiah 34:4, which we looked at a little earlier as one of the Day of the Lord passages. The only other place that talks about the heavens changing shape is in **Hebrews 1:11-12** where it talks about God rolling the heavens and earth up like an old cloak.

I'm sure astrophysicists have some interesting thoughts about what this would mean for outer space, but it's not really possible to explain this with anything naturally occurring. And it's clear the Earth Dwellers know perfectly well it isn't anything normal.

The rest of the chapter is a KEY to the End Times. We see all the people on earth hiding in caves just like Isaiah 2:19-21 predicted. The top rulers, the famous, the rich, the military brass, the powerful, as well as all the ordinary people—even slaves—hide. And they know whom they are trying to escape from. Everyone recognizes it is God the Father and the Lamb who are unleashing their wrath. And the Earth Dwellers don't think they can stand it. They're right.

Some people make a big deal where the Greek tense says the Day of Wrath "is come." Some scholars still go with the old idea that this form which is known as the "timeless" form (*aorist* for the adults) is closest to our past tense. In their mind, they think it should be written that the "Day of Wrath already came." They do this so they can make God's wrath start way back at the first seal.

But even if this were good Greek (which it's not), we already know the fifth seal martyrs under the altar were ticked because God hadn't unleashed his wrath yet. So even if it was in the past, you can't even push it back a single seal. Only people who need God's wrath to cover all future events to fit their tradition think this way.

Do you remember Jesus's prophecy we went over at the beginning of this study? We've seen this same reaction after the same events somewhere else. Keep your spot in Revelation and flip back to read Matthew 24:29–31 again. Look familiar? It should. Then look up Joel 2:30–32. Yes, indeed. It's the exact same sequence.

Both Jesus and Joel have the sun, moon, and stars darkened before God moves in a mighty way, but both of them have something happen to God's people next. Will John see the elect gathered from across the world and those who call on the Lord delivered in Israel? Let's see!

Revelation 7

The book of Revelation gives us some glimpses into the spiritual world we wouldn't otherwise have. One of those glimpses comes right here.

There are four angels in charge of the winds blowing over the whole world. And another angel commands them to wait before damaging the place.

That's seriously cool to know about how our world works. Do we need to be kind to our planet? Of course, just like we are kind to our own homes. But human beings aren't alone, we have angels helping, or hurting when necessary.

What are the wind angels waiting for? God's servants need to receive a seal on their forehead first. John doesn't give us any details about this, because the same kind of event happened long ago. Turn to **Ezekiel 9:1–11** to see how similar that time was.

In Ezekiel's day, the Spirit of God is in the process of leaving Solomon's temple, opening the way for it to be destroyed by Nebuchadnezzar, and Ezekiel sees a group of angels gathered to deal with the people of Jerusalem. Most of the people are evil (Chapter 8 showed us how deeply they loved their idols and wickedness.), but some were sighing and groaning because of the sin. These people get marked by the angel with the scribe's kit (a palette of dried ink, brush, and mixing pots).

Just like these ancient people were protected by heavenly ink on their foreheads, these future guys will be as well.

Who are the people protected? 12,000 from each of the tribes of Israel. When you read the names, you'll see both Joseph and his son Manasseh are listed. The one that's missing is Dan. We don't know why God switched these two out, but it's possible this happens because Dan was the far northern tribe that was known for its golden calf statue. Later, Dan is still a tribe who gets land appointed like the rest (Ezekiel 48:1–2), but his descendants aren't here at the transition time.

What's really exciting is that through all those years God watched over Jacob's children and made sure they will have enough men willing to serve Jesus to join this group. Benjamin nearly got wiped out way back in Judges 20:46–21:3. Most of the northern tribes were dragged off to Iran before Daniel was born (2 Kings 18:11). All kinds of enemies, from the Romans to the Nazis, tried to wipe the whole population out. But God has always kept a few alive, and he always will!

This next point is really important, so take your time to think about it.

Where are these 144,000 guys when they get sealed?

The four angels just got told not to hurt the earth until the people get sealed, so it only makes sense that they are still on earth, right?

So, John watches all that sealing action *on earth*.

Verse 9 marks a scene change and John tells us he saw it *after* he watched the sealing event. Now he returns his focus to the throne room of heaven and—my, does it look different up there!

Suddenly, instead of 24 elders, one John, souls under the altar, four living creatures, and myriads of angels, there are gobs of new humans he can tell come from every possible people group. If you know anything about history, you know the rivalries between tribes and nations are far worse than those between sports teams. Millions of people have died because they were part of the 'wrong' group. But not up in heaven.

Jesus told us he had one fold of sheep (followers) and he was going to be bringing in others to join them in John 10:6. Paul tells us it was God's mystery that the "Gentiles"—the peoples of the earth—were being united with the Jews through Jesus in Ephesians 3:3–6. Here we get to see them united for exactly this reason. Even their clothes tell us the story:

They all are wearing white robes (already), carrying palm branches, and shouting out "Salvation"—Hosanna, or, God totally owns salvation.

If you've grown up in church you've heard this word a million times, but what *is* "salvation"? If you were writing a new version of the Bible today you would probably use the word "rescue." The word wraps up the ideas of "cure," "rescue," and "restore" all into one. And this hosanna goes back to Psalm 118:25–26 which says the stone the builders rejected becomes the most important in the building (Jesus told people this was talking about him Matthew 21:42).

This heavenly event is almost exactly like the events of Palm Sunday. Except, unlike the Psalm 118 prediction (verse 27) and Jesus's first coming to earth, the next event will not be Jesus's sacrifice, but him becoming king of kings.

And in heaven there won't be any need for stones to cry out (Luke 19:40); all the angels, the elders, and the living creatures join the masses of human praise. It's a good thing we'll all have immortal eardrums for this!

Verses 13–14 are some of the funniest in the Bible (and there is some funny stuff, check out Psalm 78:65–66 for more.) Here's John. He's wise and old, but he's still only been in heaven for a few minutes. Why in the world is the elder asking John who these people are? No wonder John turns it around to ask the elder to tell us.

The elder's response is a KEY to the End Times. These people come out of massive persecution and have washed their robes in the Lamb's blood. They now live with God and will never be hungry, thirsty, or exposed to the sun's heat again. Jesus will lead them to living water and the Father will wipe all their tears away.

Remember, in this chapter, we were watching to see whether the elect would be gathered and those who call on the Lord delivered in Israel. Did we find these missing pieces? That's what chapter 7 was all about!

Revelation 8

OK, it's time for the seventh seal to get broken. This isn't just any seal, it's the last one in the way of the Lamb opening and owning the scroll and whatever it stands for. With the crack of this little circle, history enters a new era.

The whole multitude in heaven gets it. They wait. Silently. What's coming next must happen and it will be good that it does, but it isn't going to be pretty.

First, a set of seven angels are equipped with trumpets. Then an angel takes one of those censors and collects all the prayers from the altar. You remember what some of those prayers are, right? "How long until you avenge our murders, God!" It's time to answer all these prayers, so the angel throws the whole thing down to earth causing another earthquake.

Some people assume all the events of God's wrath on the wicked happen really quickly. They believe the trumpets we are about to study describe the same events as the seals we already looked at plus the bowls in chapter 16. But if you let the Bible speak for itself, you don't find these events matching up at all. In fact, like the plagues God sent on Egypt long ago, they keep getting worse and worse.

Now it's time for the trumpeters to start their work causing:

- Trumpet 1: Hail, fire, and blood. 1/3 of trees burnt up.
- Trumpet 2: "Mountain of fire" flung in the sea. 1/3 of the ocean turned to blood, killing 1/3 of sea creatures and sinking 1/3 of the ships. ("As

it were" or "like" tells us this wasn't really a mountain, but it was the closest visual John could give to describe what he saw.)

- Trumpet 3: "Wormwood" star falls on 1/3 of the rivers and water springs, poisoning them so lots of people die.
- Trumpet 4: Sun, moon, and stars darkened for 1/3 of the time.

Just before the chapter ends and we move to the rest of the trumpets, something new happens. We've never seen this before and there isn't anything like it in the whole rest of the Bible. While God sends angels to talk to his own people, like Daniel, Joseph, and even disobedient Israel (Judges 2:1–3), he's never used heavenly messengers to talk to the people on earth like this before.

Why now? Do you know how Jesus gets his message out most of the time? Through his people. Paul says this straight out in 2 Corinthians 5:18–20. And when Cornelius had pleased God so much he wanted him and his family to hear about Jesus, he sent him an angel—but not with the gospel, just directions to where to find Peter (Acts 10:3–7).

There are still 144,000 Israelites on earth, but how are they going to give a global message? They will have been totally canceled from the internet and it's not like the media is going to feature an ad even if they could afford one. So God uses an angel to bypass those who hate him and warn everyone they *ain't seen nothing yet.*

Revelation 9

Woe #1 Trumpet five opens with a star who gets a key to a place we've never heard of before, but we'll see it again. You might have heard of the bottomless pit, and it's fascinating to think about how this could work considering the nature of gravity.

If you could have a hole punched through the center of the earth you'll end up with a space where nothing ever hits the bottom. And if something gets thrown down this shaft, after a lot of falling it would continue its momentum past the core to nearly reach the other side before getting pulled back towards the center. This would keep happening until the thing thrown in eventually ended up in limbo, stuck floating right at the core of the earth.

And what was stuck in this place? Bugs. Not your everyday creepy crawlies, these are locusts, and even in the normal world, such insects are horrible. If you read Laura Ingalls Wilder's account of a year experiencing these pests in her book *On the Banks of Plum Creek* you'll see how devastating they were in America long ago. And the Middle East experiences swarms all too often.

These locusts in Revelation aren't plant-eating insects, though. In fact, they are commanded not to hurt anything green. Instead, they have scorpion tails and a single assignment:

Make life feel worse than death for anyone that doesn't have God's seal of protection on them.

Lots of people have made guesses about what these locust/scorpions/horses with all that armor and hair "like women" really are. These guesses usually look silly years later. But this is a great point to stop and think about the predicament John was in.

Here you have a first-century guy. Remember, John was one of Jesus's disciples. Picture fishing boats, Roman palaces, sandals, and barley loaves for lunch. Then picture a future society at least as complex as ours. And that's before we add all the spiritual beings like these demon bugs into the mix. And John tells us what he sees is a "vision," which is why he sees Jesus as a wooly young sheep with a bunch of horns and eyes while looking like he got slaughtered.

So, it's quite likely people watching this in real life will recognize these things match John's description. I also think a bunch of us are going to be going, "Oh! So *that's* what he meant!"

Back to people having ideas about what these bugs are. Many people assume they are something designed by humans—like tanks. But remember, they had been locked away in the Bottomless Pit. And they have a king, who is called the angel of the abyss and whose name, Apollyon, means Destroyer.

Psalm 35:5–6 asks God to use an angel to hurt the bad guys. In 1 Chronicles 21:15–16 God sends a destroying angel to make 70,000 Jewish soldiers drop dead of plague when David messed up. Isaiah 37:36 tells how God's angel wiped out 150,000 enemy soldiers. God's destroying angel could even be assigned to give a single jerk a horrible death (Acts 12:23). Hebrews 11:28 tells us the way God killed the firstborn of Egypt was with a destroyer.

This Apollyon is one bad dude who spends most of his time locked up, so we always assume he's a demon. But he still has to follow God's orders, only killing those he is allowed to, or here in Revelation only making the Earth Dwellers *wish* they were dead. Now, if the idea of God using a demon on purpose seems crazy to you, look at how a prophet tells the kings of Israel and Judah this is exactly what God did in **1 Kings 22:19–23**. It's mind-blowing, but God sent this spirit to lie *for God's purposes.*

Can we know for sure this Destroyer king is the same spirit messenger as in the Old Testament? Not really. But he and his hordes fit in well with those other events.

Interestingly, this is one of the points where Jesus gives us a specific timeframe. This plague of scorpion pain will last for five months. Whatever timeline ends up playing out for the transfer of power from the Earth Dwellers to Jesus has to fit this block into it.

Woe #2 starts in **verse 13** when the sixth angel blows his trumpet. A voice comes out of God's altar and tells the trumpet angel what to do. He is to release four angels that were tied up in the river that flows by Babylon. These have to be evil angels to be tied up like this, but God has held them for exactly this time.

I have no idea why John gets so specific about the "hour, and day, and month, and year." Usually, God says way less than we could wish to save the poor scribes from having to use more ink and parchment. There is even some question whether these times are pointing at an exact moment or giving them the total length of time (13 months, 25 hours) to do their deed.

Whichever way this works out, these four dudes collect an army of 200 million to help them. And this army has some seriously scary horses. Unlike the bug versions, these guys don't just make people wish they were dead; they drop one-third of all the people on earth dead with their breath.

Like the earlier bug-horses, lots of people have ideas about this army. At the moment it's popular to think they are a real human army. No matter how much you shoehorn the way those horses are described into what a human army could be outfitted with, they do not look like modern military equipment. Lion heads? Tails like serpents with heads? Really? And there is no sign here of them being led by any kind of conqueror. God sent their spirit leaders with one purpose. To hurt the Earth Dwellers who defied him. And that they do quite well.

Verses 20–21 are a KEY to why God sends this kind of destruction on the earth. We know Jesus already rescued his people from their tribulation. There aren't Christians around to persecute (or not many), but everyone on earth knows perfectly well God is real, Jesus is powerful, and he deserves their worship and honor.

But the Earth Dwellers won't. They love their evil. They would rather worship demons and the empty things they have made with their own hands. They want to murder the people they hate, follow the occult and take drugs (the Greek word used here means both magic and mind-altering drugs since these things always walk hand in hand), use people, and steal.

Revelation 10

Remember how chapter 7 slowed the timeline down after the sixth seal to focus on the 144,000 and the great multitude instead of breaking the seals? This chapter and most of the next four give us another pause like that, and it starts after the sixth trumpet.

Here John watches as a "mighty angel" descends to earth. He may be wearing stuff you might see on a little girl's cartoon, but his face and feet are fiery bright. He's no sissy! And he's so huge he stands with one foot on dry land and the other in the ocean.

Why in the world did God bother to tell us about the seven thunders but not let us know what they said? We cannot know for sure since he didn't tell us, but it does sound like an eyewitness journal entry. When a story is all neat and tidy the investigators start getting really suspicious. John tells us about lots of things he didn't understand. Now his blow-by-blow account is so detailed he tells us he heard a message too top secret to pass on.

Verse 6 has been used by a lot of preachers for a long time to make an extraordinary case about time itself. If they had used a modern version this wouldn't have been confusing, but the KJV says the angel swore "that there should be time no longer." They would use this phrase to talk about heaven having no flow of time in it, but we'll see in Revelation 22:2 how impossible this is. All the angel promised was that there wouldn't be any more delay. Time is up!

He finishes his sentence by announcing that the "Mystery of God" is about to be finished as the seventh trumpet sounds. What is this "mystery" or "secret"? Let's look ahead and see. In Revelation 11:15 we finally hear the sound of the seventh trumpet. And the answer is announced by heavenly voices saying the kingdoms of earth are going to be ruled from that point on by God the Father and Jesus Christ.

God's mysteries aren't like a Sherlock Holmes story. If we are paying attention to his prophets we can figure out what he's planning just fine. Daniel had told us long before that the Son of Man would take over as king of the whole world. Another of God's mysteries is that Jesus would add people from every people group on earth into his kingdom (Romans 16:25–26). But he had told Abraham and the prophets this long before (Galatians 3:8).

John's scroll-snack is fun to think about. Have you ever eaten baklava? It's a dessert made from honey and nuts layered in paper-thin phyllo pastry. If you make it yourself, you could roll the sheets into a scroll a lot like this—someone good with a brush could even write words on the dough! But the mighty-angel-baked one John eats has something odd about it. The taste is sweet, but it messes up his tummy.

And if I had to realize in the very core of my being just how bad it's going to get for the Earth Dwellers, I would get a stomach ache too. Ezekiel got to eat a scroll like this in **Ezekiel 3:1–4**. He is told right away it will give him words to share with his people. And John is told in **verse 11** that he has to prophesy about all kinds of people. Neither got to quietly watch events unfold; they were called to announce them before they happened, even though their news is devastating.

Revelation 11

We're still in the pause that started with the mighty angel; the chapter break is just there to give people a place to quit for the day if they want. So, John gets handed a measuring stick and told to measure the temple, altar, *and* the people who worship, but I doubt he was checking whether anyone was as tall as Goliath! In fact, we never hear if John actually tests the size of that temple, probably because his attention is so quickly pulled away. (Don't worry; he'll get to measure again when it's time for the place of worship to last forever!)

First, John was to leave out the courtyard of the temple because it and the rest of Jerusalem are going to be overrun by the people of earth for 42 months. These people won't just walk around; they will *trample* God's city and the temple area. This is not a pretty picture of how they treat what God calls holy.

It's been a while since we've had a time measure like this, but how many years does 42 months work out to? Three and a half. We've seen this before, except Daniel used "time, times, and half a time." Bible scholars aren't even sure which part of the full seven-year "week" to connect these next events with. Good, logical cases can be made for the temple to be trampled and the ministry of the prophets we read about next being either the first or second half of the seven years.

Personally, I don't even think it's necessary for them to fit into these two possible timeframes. Perhaps the trampling and witnessing (which do seem to be connected) start somewhere after the week begins but before the Abomination of Desolation. I think they are finished prophesying when the angel announces the three Woes in 8:10. Whatever the timeframe is, wise Bible students hold their ideas loosely, expecting to find out a lot more when the real events happen.

These two prophets are some of the most interesting characters in prophecy. They start right out setting us a puzzle about who they could be, and it takes careful digging in the Old Testament to find out what John says they are.

To find the "two olive trees" you have to turn back to **Zechariah 4:2–3, 11–14**. These 'trees' supply the heavenly menorah with oil and stand in front of the Lord of the whole earth. But that's all Zechariah ever found out. Now

John is going to see them a lot more clearly.

First, they are humans. Angels can't leave dead bodies around. And these guys are prophets, witnessing to the Earth Dwellers for 1,260 days. If you use a 360-day calendar this works out to exactly 3 1/2 years. They spend this time preaching in Jerusalem, the same city where Jesus was tortured to death (**verse 8**). This would give the Jews the greatest chance to hear them in person—or get fried.

'Cause these aren't your typical street preachers. Can you imagine going to the big city and hearing someone shouting about how people have rebelled against God? Some thug lumbers up to them and—wham-bam—fire flies out of their mouths and burns him to a crisp. That would get your attention! And, to prove they are legit prophets warning people about what God really says, they stop the rain, turn water to blood, and bring on who-knows-what other plagues.

So we know:

- These are mortal humans
- They were already standing before God hundreds of years before Jesus was born
- They control plagues like drought and turn water to blood

You can guess which people most Bible teachers think these guys are. Elijah asked God to stop it from raining on earth for exactly three years and six months (James 5:17). Moses turned water into blood and brought all kinds of other plagues long ago.

Is the answer this easy? First, Hebrews 9:27 tells us our mortal bodies only die once. Jesus and others brought people back from the dead, but it was much more like waking out of a super-deep sleep since the longest any of them had been separated from their bodies was the four days Lazarus was buried. Everyone else was raised within hours and they all went on to die ordinary deaths at some point.

Second, Jesus can't be killed again; he conquered the Last Enemy: Death. And his people get immortal bodies that can't be destroyed when they are resurrected (1 Corinthians 15:53–54).

For me, Elijah is a perfect candidate. Malachi predicted he would come back before the great and dreadful Day of the Lord (4:5). Like lots of prophecies, there was a 'type' of Elijah when Jesus first came, but that guy wasn't actually the Old Testament prophet; we get to hear all about John the Baptist's birth!

And even if we believed in reincarnation (which the Bible teaches isn't real: Hebrews 9:27; Genesis 3:19), Elijah never left his mortal body behind to come back as anyone else. He rose on a whirlwind out of Elisha's sight (2 Kings 2:11), so he could still be killable as these men are. But Moses' body got buried by the archangel Michael (Jude 1:9), so he was separated from his mortal body long ago.

There is another prophet that we know very little about except that he took his body with him to heaven. Enoch "walked with God" and wasn't there Hebrbecause God took him (Genesis 5:24). We also know he was a prophet because of what Jude told us (Jude 1:14–15). But we don't have any record of him casting plagues on the bad guys.

So, can we know for sure who these ancient men are? No. God didn't need us to know, but it is fun to try to puzzle together.

Verse 7 introduces—finally—one of the key characters of the End of history. We saw him lots of times with Jesus's and Daniel's predictions, but John had avoided mentioning him until here. "The beast" that comes out of the bottomless pit is going to murder God's prophets.

No one thinks this is one of the locust horses or Apollyon. A few think the beast is Satan himself, but most teachers believe this is the Little Horn, the Antichrist. Since the two witnesses are real humans and they really die, it makes sense that their murderer would be someone with a physical body too. He is powerful in the spiritual realm, though, since he doesn't get fried by the witnesses or die of any of the plagues they can unleash.

But even the two witnesses' death is part of God's plan. The Beast isn't allowed to kill them until God decides they have done all the preaching they need to. He lets things get deadly for them, but only because he's about to let them retire forever.

Verses 8–10 record the only time in the whole book of Revelation the Earth

Dwellers are ever happy. All across the globe, people from every demographic spend the next three days watching the mangled bodies of the witnesses. This by itself has made modern preachers sit up and wonder how much time we have left. A single century ago the thought of everyone everywhere watching this in real time was fantasy. Today we watch all kinds of live cams. It's not science fiction anymore; it's ordinary.

Can you imagine this kind of celebration? Let's throw a party as we watch the rotting bodies of the guys who wanted us to repent and honor the real God. Hurrah, the Beast we like is stronger than the Creator we hate! One verse. Three and a half days. That's all the happiness they'll ever get for the rest of eternity.

And then God steps in. The Holy Spirit resurrects his witnesses and scares the liver out of the Earth Dwellers. Everyone hears the mighty voice calling them to "Come on up!" (This time the command is plural in Greek since there are two of them.) They rise into heaven like Jesus did, just in time to avoid the great earthquake that squashes a bunch of people.

Why John mentions 7,000 dying is a puzzle; sadly, a "great" earthquake usually kills many more people than that. It could be a bunch of important leaders or have some symbolic meaning. Or it could just be that the buildings in Jerusalem are really well designed.

What we do know is the Earth Dwellers give God glory for all these things. This doesn't have to mean they submit to him, but no one can continue thinking God isn't real or that these events were all accidents. We also know some people *do* turn to worship God no matter the cost.

For a chapter and a half, we've been focusing on a few characters, but in **verse 14** we whip right back into the main timeline of events. It seems that the witnesses' violent departure from earth was the second woe, even though their assignment lasted for 3 1/2 years.

Now it's time for the last of the three woes, and if the first two affected so many people, what's coming next?

The end of this chapter marks another KEY, and it's a pivot point. **Verses 15–19** move us back to the throne room of heaven. The seventh angel blows his trumpet, but nothing bad happens on earth right away. Instead, a major proclamation is made in the heavenlies.

Lots of voices announce God and his Messiah are now king of all the countries on earth. The 24 elders join the praise, saying that God has "begun to reign." They tell us that even though the Earth Dwellers got mad as hell, God's wrath is even worse. They also note that this is the time when God gives rewards and punishments.

John never watches the award ceremony for God's people—perhaps because he would be embarrassed to watch himself get buried in treasure—but we know it happens in connection with this trumpet.

To get a glimpse of what it is like to experience this heavenly-citizen judgment we have to look at what Paul told us in **1 Corinthians 3:10–16**. Paul tells us he helped lay the only house foundation that can last, Jesus Christ. If you have this, you're in the club; if you don't, you're lost.

But each of us spends our mortal lives building onto this foundation with all kinds of materials. Paul doesn't tell us what marks the difference between the flammable stuff and the expensive, forever stuff. But when it comes time for this judgment, finding out which one you built with is as easy as calling in a pyrotechnic angel.

I want to live so I receive my reward and all the eternal VIP perks that go along with a life well-lived. But if you know someone who doesn't choose Jesus until the last opportunity, like the thief on the cross did, don't feel too bad for them. Being a member of God's family is a perk that's out of this world. But, if you are young and healthy and can choose how to live your life—I suggest you go for the total upgrade; you won't ever regret it!

And, whatever you do, don't let God's judgment terrify you too much. **Romans 14:4** warns us not to judge other Christians because their Master, God, can vindicate them. And, just a chapter after his solemn explanation of how our accomplishments could end up burnt to a crisp, Paul tells us in **1 Corinthians 4:3–5** that he doesn't worry about what other people think of his work, or even whether he is pleased with it, God is the only Judge who matters. Jesus will expose all our motives and hidden thinking, but, for his people, this means every one of us will receive praise from God.

This concept is a KEY for the entire Christian life. If I really belong to God, he isn't looking for any chance he can find to yell at me. His goal is to reward and praise me because he is a loving Father, not an ogre.

Next, we get a rare glimpse into the deepest parts of heaven as it exists now. Remember, Moses was told to make everything like the real version. The earthly ones were always just shadowy copies of the real deal (Hebrews 8:5). We already saw the altar, but in the worship God had the Jews set up, the altar was outside the temple in the middle of the courtyard. Now we get to see all the way through to the back of the real temple—no doors, no veil. Jesus's death tore apart the veil in Jerusalem, and now even in heaven nothing is closed off from God's people.

Take a minute to read **Hebrews 10:19–23**. Isn't this exciting stuff?

Just before the end of the chapter, though, we are reminded that as amazing as all this is for us, it's devastating for those who refuse to honor Jesus. This last trumpet unleashes another earthquake and a great hail.

We're going to see more hail. If you don't know anyone who's been through a bad storm, you could read what it was like for Laura Ingalls Wilder in her book *The First Four Years*. An everyday hailstorm can destroy a year's crop in minutes. And the one the trumpet sound causes was no ordinary storm.

Revelation 12

We already had a long break from the flow of time in the last two chapters and now we're about to plunge into a section that lasts for three more chapters before we get back to the main timeline! You can see why this gets confusing, even for adults.

Not only are these scenes out of sequence, pretty much all the things John sees at this point switch from realistic to symbolic. Up until now, you could make a movie of the events John saw—you would just need some spectacular special effects and CG horse riders. But at this point, it gets much more like Daniel's four-beast visions than a Michael Bay movie.

Now John steps back and introduces us to the main characters at the time of the transfer of power to Jesus. And this first one is a strange vision; it's one of two important "women" in Revelation. Neither seems to be any single real woman. Let's see if we can make a decent guess about what John is being shown.

Christianity doesn't have a goddess, but this lady sounds powerful and beautiful. The sun, moon, and stars remind us of what Joseph dreamed about as a teenager that his father Jacob interpreted as representing their family (Genesis 37:9–10). And this lady gives birth to a baby who is to rule the nations with an "iron rod" and is taken up to be safe with God. This baby sounds a lot like Jesus, whose human body is from Jacob's family. So, it's an easy step to assume this woman represents all of Israel from her beginning to the time of the end.

And it also fits right in with other prophecies like Joel 2:32 for Israel to be protected. The new thing we learn here is that these people will be kept safe hiding in the wilderness for 1,260 days, in other words, God will provide them a refuge for 3 1/2 years.

Next comes the "great red dragon" to try to destroy the baby and the woman. This one is easy. Satan certainly tried to wipe out Jesus and he is both God and Israel's enemy. This is an even easier connection to make since we first met Satan when he showed up as a serpent in the Garden of Eden. Now he's a ginormous version of the same wily character.

The first part of **verse 4** is a flash of light into the spiritual world. God knows better than to terrify us or let us obsess about his angels and the ones who fell, but he gives us enough to go on. Here we get a piece of what happened when Lucifer (Bringer of Light, the Morning Star) rebelled against God: his 'tail' caused one out of three of the other stars to fall with him.

This tells us that for every demon (fallen angel) there are two angels who stayed faithful to God. There are twice as many good ones as bad! But since we know there are myriads of angels (5:11) there are vast numbers of Satan's followers too.

Next, we back up a little more to focus on this dragon, Satan.

Verses 7–8 are amazing if you stop to think for a minute. Right up until the time of this war Satan and his demons still have places in heaven. What?! You can see a bit of how this works in Job 1–2 where Satan presents himself before God. Interestingly, when it's time for them to be thrown out, God doesn't just shove them out himself, he has his good angels fight them. Demons can fight dirty, but they are outnumbered two to one, and being good doesn't make you weak, so, Michael, the chief angel, gets the job done.

In **Luke 10:18** Jesus talks about having seen Satan fall like a star from heaven in the past when his disciple reported their success casting out demons, and the rest of the chapter seems like it could picture all of Christian history if you only looked at it loosely. But when you keep reading to the end of the chapter you see the dragon realizes he's about to be fully conquered only after the woman is hidden in the wilderness and all the people he can hurt are the rest of her children (verse 17).

Verse 10 is something you'll want to think about as you grow up. Satan does a lot of things to try to damage us: he lies, he tempts, he hurts. But to accuse us is one of the most horrible because if we listen to him, we start to believe all the disgusting things he tells God about us. We have washed our robes in Jesus's blood; he has made us clean and holy. Satan is the one who keeps trying to make us feel ugly and sinful. **Verse 11** gives us the solution for helping us escape from Satan's temptations and lies. It's one of the most powerful for you (and all Christians) to have memorized and buried deep in your heart to help you through whatever hard times life brings.

In many ways, this is one of those double prophecies. Jesus already won and gives us salvation and strength and expands his kingdom. He's been doing this for nearly 2,000 years. But there is a time coming when these things will be ultimately fulfilled and Satan won't have any more power to lie or hurt people. That has not yet happened.

Verses 12 and 17 give us another KEY to End Time events. We saw Jesus finally show his anger at the end of chapter 6. Here we see Satan furious because he knows he's almost out of time, so he's boiling hot and determined to hurt as many of God's people as he possibly can—because he knows he can never actually win against God.

As we get pulled back to the characters we saw earlier, the Dragon/Serpent chases after the woman again. This time we see how she manages to escape as God gives her eagle wings to fly into "her place." And, in case we're tempted to think this is a long symbolic time, we get told she stays in the wilderness for three and a half "times" just like before.

I really love **verses 15–16**. There is nothing else like this in the Bible, and it doesn't actually end up changing any events, but the thought is majorly cool. The dragon wants to flush out the woman (pun intended), so he sends a flash flood into the wilderness area he knows she has to be in. Not fire, like a self-respecting dragon, but water. Some guess this might be because God once wiped out all of Satan's human followers with a flood? We don't really know.

Anyway, who rescues the woman? A boat? An angel? Nope. The earth itself opens up to "swallow" all the water and leave her safe and dry. There is one other account of the earth opening up and swallowing stuff, but that time the earth protected Moses from a group of arrogant, rebellious Israelites (Numbers 26:10).

There are a handful of places in the Bible where the earth or ground talks to God about the sin of the people living on it. This time Planet Earth has had enough and won't let Satan wipe out God's protected people. (You might pay attention to how the Israelis right now are restoring and caring for their land even when they don't belong to Jesus yet.)

It's a rather fuzzy prophecy by itself, but now is a good time to read **Isaiah 26**. It's from Israel's perspective and you'll want to especially focus on what he says in **verses 17–21**. These word pictures sound like both Revelation 12 and what Jesus said about future events being similar to a woman getting ready to have her child. Pay attention to the order of events: pregnancy, resurrection, hiding God's people, God's judgment on the wicked. Have we seen this sequence before?

Revelation 13

We are about halfway through the pause in John's timeline narrative and he's finally going to introduce us properly to the big bad guy players on earth.

You remember when Daniel was shown how the different nations would rise and fall? They were compared to beasts with characteristics fitting their style of conquering and ruling. Daniel's last beast wasn't really described except as "terrible," and now it's time to see why that was a reasonable way to put it.

This animal comes out of the sea just like Daniel's (7:2–3) and it looks a lot like the ones he had described—except mixed all together. The leopard, lion, and bear are all blended into one new beast which has seven heads and ten crowned horns.

Remember, in Revelation 12:3 the Dragon, Satan, is described as having the same number of heads and horns. If this one ends up being the same beast as in chapter 17, we'll find out the "seven heads" are seven mountains. These heads have names on them that are "blasphemous." We use this big word when we talk about someone saying things you should never say about God (calling him bad) or about yourself (calling yourself god).

And we've already met the 10 toes or horns. We'll see more about what happens with them soon, but remember, Daniel saw these horns and how the Little Horn came up afterward.

John's vision is taking us back to the last evil earthly government and trying to describe it. We don't yet know whether this beast will rule over every bit of dry land on earth, but you can see how if you're trying to describe something anywhere close to being global, it's going to be hard to put into Bible-time words!

This beast is given its power straight from the Dragon. And Satan has a lot of power to give it!

Verse 3 doesn't tell us which of the heads gets mortally wounded, but since we never hear about any of the others in the whole Bible this has to mean the Little Horn, the Lawless Antichrist. Why switch from a horn to the head it's on? If you cut off an animal's horn it doesn't get a deadly wound.

And here's something else to keep in mind when you're thinking about a government. From the time of the Pharaohs and Assyrians to the Roman and Chinese emperors, and even modern dictators, this has been true: a single, human leader becomes the face of the government. Statues, paintings, and worship have always been about the one person at the top of the pile for these civilizations.

And this particular thing happening to a single guy whose name can be the "Anti-Christ" makes sense. Jesus Christ really did die and rise again under his own power. While Satan is a creature with limited power, he does have a lot of it. He knows what causes people to die; he could stop the process for his minion, allowing his God-designed body to heal itself.

Satan is always mimicking God. For him to use an assassination attempt or some other violent event to copy Jesus's power over death would be something he wants to do for all kinds of reasons. The end of **verse 3** and the next verse shows us one of the biggest of these reasons.

The people of the earth are watching this violence happen and then they see their powerful ruler healed from what would have killed any of them. Just as they will recognize the sun, moon, and stars are controlled by Jesus, here they recognize the Dragon was the one who rescued the Beast from death.

And this time they are willing to worship him and his servant, the Beast.

The questions they ask themselves here form a KEY to the End Times. "Who is like the beast? Who can make war with him?" The first question tells us Jesus hasn't burst on the scene yet. He is more than a match for this almost-dying ruler. He did die and rose three days later!

And by seeing the people asking who could wage war against the Beast, it tells us people had been fighting him. Other people would have still liked to resist him, but now they become too scared to try. Remember how the first two horsemen represented "conquering" and "war"? The Beast is conquering, but the world doesn't just let him take over their countries without a fight.

I kind of wonder whether that deadly wound was given to him by one of the countries that didn't want the Beast as their master. It's a guess, but as good as any.

Now we get to a time marker. This Beast-Antichrist is given 42 months to rule. Remember what that works out to in years? Yes, indeed, 3 1/2 years. This near-death experience marks the middle of the 70th Week of Daniel and we're about to see the Abomination of Desolation in full detail.

First, the Beast shows just how mouthy he can be. This is one of the clearest things we know about this puppet of Satan. No one has ever talked smack about God worse than this dude. Not only do his words tear down God, he speaks out against God's tabernacle and even people who have already died and gone to heaven.

In 2020 we saw statues torn down because some people believed those who were being honored by these monuments were actually bad guys not worth remembering. The Beast is going to do something like this and far worse.

Satan and his people do not have any actual power to hurt God and those in heaven with their words, but Satan knows how to hurt God at his heart: hurt the mortal people he loves. So **verse 7** tells us one of the saddest and most horrible things in history. The goal of this conquering pseudo-god will be to fight against God's people. And he is going to win.

This kind of persecution has happened, and is happening, in countries around the world, but never before everywhere on earth at the same time with this ferocity. The last part of **verse 7** tells us there won't be any place left that's safe for God's people. We already know some will be hidden by God in the wilderness to the east of Israel, and Paul has told us there will be survivors (1 Thessalonians 4:17), but Jesus also told us if these days weren't "cut short" none of the elect would make it (Matthew 24:22).

All of this is terrifying, and without God's help, we could be crushed under the weight of fear. But **verses 9–10** tell us what to pay attention to: what goes around, comes around. Jesus isn't about to let Satan & Co. get away with this, and he is far, far greater. We're going to see in a few chapters just how easy it is for Jesus to squash this guy like a bug. But remember, God waits until enough of his people get murdered before it's time to make his own war (6:11).

The rest of the chapter tells us some extraordinary things about the Beast's kingdom. First, we meet his spokesman, someone or something that looks like a lamb but talks like a dragon. He's got just as much power, but he doesn't want the worship for himself, he turns the people to worship the once mostly-dead Beast.

This Lamb-Dragon doesn't show up anywhere else in the Bible, but it's easy to see what he pictures. Remember, Satan is the Great Fake and rebelled because he wanted to be "like the Most High." (**Isaiah 14:14**). One of the most important things about the real God is that he exists in three persons: the Father, the Son, and the Holy Spirit.

Satan is one angel, but with his deadly-wound Beast and this Lamb-Dragon, it feels like a trinity—an unholy and limited one.

There are two terrible and important things this Lamb-Dragon does. He takes a page out of the two witnesses' book and brings down fire out of heaven—just like a real prophet. He can do all kinds of things that point to the first Beast—if he's in his presence. And he calls on the Earth Dwellers to make an image of the Beast.

Remember how Antiochus Epiphanies had a statue of himself placed in God's temple? That, and the disgusting sacrifices and worship rituals are what the first, ancient Abomination of Desolation was.

We aren't told what the Earth Dwellers do in their worship, but considering what we know about pagan worship, I'm glad John wasn't told to write down the details!

Here's where it gets super weird. Unless this idol is some kind of mech, the Lamb-Dragon has the power to breathe life into it, like something out of a sci-fi movie. We aren't told the image can move around, but it can speak for itself, and it does something that causes those who refuse to worship it to be killed.

The other thing the Lamb-Dragon directs the Earth Dwellers to do is give people the Mark of the Beast. This is one KEY to the End Times lots of people know about, but it still can be awfully confusing. It's extra scary to think you could get this somehow by accident. But does the Bible say you could get the Mark without knowing it?

Let's look at what John tells us:

- People have it set in their forehead or hand
- It is used to allow buying and selling
- The Beast's number, 666, is one of the possibilities for people to get

That's it. Or is it? If you skip ahead just a few verses to Revelation 14:9–11, you'll see an angel flies through the sky warning that anyone who gets this is doomed to eternal torment. It is used as a literal mark that declares you have rejected the worship of God. There's no second chance on this decision.

Do you think God would let any of his children accidentally take something that forces them to worship the Antichrist and end up in hell? Not a chance.

Jesus told his Father he'd never lost one soul except for Judas Iscariot who didn't really belong to him in the first place (John 17:12). He also tells us in John 6:37–40 that he will raise all of his people on the Last Day.

Until you've seen a series of angels making global announcements for God, you don't have to worry about someone slipping you the Mark of the Beast.

But when this time comes, there will be tremendous pressure to worship the Beast. Without that mark, you are out of business and can't even buy toilet paper. What's incredible is that we will see there are mortal people who are so ornery they refuse even this and manage to survive somehow.

Revelation 14

Next scene: After a chapter of the biggest bad guys of all time, John gives us a break to visit the Lamb and his followers. Since we already know who this is, we aren't given any details about him except for where he is.

John sees the Lamb on God's eternally chosen hill of Mount Zion—at least for a minute. Jesus is with his followers, and, if we hadn't been told their number, we would think they were brand new characters. But there's only one other time in the Bible a group of 144,000 shows up, and that's the Israelis from all the tribes. Now we find out the "seal" they got in their foreheads back in Chapter 7 was God the Father's name. So, here are all these guys who follow Jesus everywhere, but they have the Father's name on them. This reminds us a bit of what 1 Corinthians 15:28 teaches us.

Even though we start on earth, the scene quickly moves up to heaven where many voices and people with harps start to sing. Did you know this is the only place we hear about anyone besides the 24 elders having harps in heaven? You've probably seen drawings of people with halos sitting on clouds and strumming harps. We *do* get to ride up on clouds, and these people *do* play harps, but halos are an artistic addition and no one is going to force you to sit around plunking strings—unless you want to. And when you add in subwoofers like the voice of "thunder" it's hardly sissy up there!

Many couples have something they call "their song." It may be loved by thousands, but it's one that means something extra special to the two of them.

These guys have a song so special no one else gets to sing it to God. And, it's not that different from a love song since these guys would rather follow Jesus wherever he goes than marry and live a normal life.

"Firstfruits" is an important concept in the Bible. If you farm, you don't collect all the food at the same time; some of it ripens before the rest, or you start harvesting at one edge of the field. The rule was, the way to show God you were grateful for his care over your farm was to give him this first part. Even your animals were to have their first lamb given as sacrifices to God.

These men aren't burnt on an altar, but they are compared to these offerings of Israel's best. Even mentioning that they never lie and are blameless fits the kind of offering they were to bring. God didn't want a damaged animal offered to him because the brokenness of their bodies was a picture of how sin breaks our souls.

Verse 6 shifts scenes again but is probably connected to the last one because we get to see more angels doing the work God's prophets and followers have done throughout most of history. They fly across the sky to every country and people group on the planet. If even the 144,000 and the two witnesses are up in heaven at this point, it's not surprising God uses a kind of media no country can shut down.

The first angel preaches the Good News that lasts forever. Let's break down what he announces:

- God is the one who deserves glory and respect because he's the one bringing judgment on sin
- God deserves worship for creating the whole universe

The next angel introduces us to the last big 'character' we meet, the city of the Lawless One and center of false worship: Babylon.

People do commit "fornication," or all kinds of sexual sin, but this probably has more to do with what God talked about through the prophet Hosea. When we worship and honor anything the way we are supposed to worship and serve God, it is a lot like someone who is married living with another person instead. God hurts, and it hurts us. And this evil makes him seriously ticked—enough to warn he's going to destroy the whole city.

In the last chapter, we already talked about the third angel's message. Worshipping the Beast, his image, and getting his mark on your body spells your eternal doom. The angel goes on to give us a terrifying picture of what eternal punishment looks like. Not only will you die a horrible death, that first death is just the beginning of your misery.

Pictures of this kind of punishment do two things: they help us remember why sharing about God as Creator, Judge, and Rescuer is so important today. And it helps us never give up following Jesus no matter how tough it gets. Nothing the Earth Dwellers can do to us is as bad as what God could do to us!

Jesus told us this concept straight out in **Matthew 10:28**. Don't be afraid of people who can only kill your body and then have no more power over you. Fear God who has the power to throw your eternal soul into hell forever.

The question is: Do I really believe Jesus is going to keep his promise to bring justice on everyone?

Next, in **verse 13**, John gets a message from heaven directly for us. At the point the angels present their message this is the only hope for people who choose Jesus over the Beast: Death equals rest and reward for those in the Master. We know some mortals survive into Jesus's reign, but from everything we've seen, the Beast is going to do everything he can to destroy anyone who resists him.

All these messages remind us there are fates far worse than a Christian's death.

This last vision with symbolic angels is one that puzzles everyone. Is this harvest scene a recap of everything that's happened, or something new? And, if we *can* make heads or tails of it, do we learn anything new about the timeline of Revelation or not? I'll share my ideas, but there is a lot here that feels more like one of Jesus's parables, and wise Bible students are careful not to push things in such stories too far. Let's see what's going on.

First, who is this dude on the cloud?

Did you know this is the only place in the Bible that talks about anyone *sitting* on a cloud? And this isn't just anyone sitting there; it's the "Son of Man." Daniel talked a lot like this in 7:13 where the Son of Man comes to the

Ancient of Days to receive an eternal kingdom. And in **Isaiah 19:1** he warns Egypt that Yahweh is riding on a swift cloud to judge them.

But some scholars point out that the next sickle wielder is called "another" angel, so they figure this Son of Man is an angel. I find this hard to swallow since no angel was ever called "son of man." We've had plenty of angels earlier in the chapter, so it makes more sense to me for the word "another" to be referring to the angels we've already read about.

Some translations make this "a" son of man, so it could be more like any human being. God was fond of calling his prophet Ezekiel "son of man," constantly reminding us all the prophet was just a mortal. But this cloud-sitter doesn't act like an ordinary Joe. He's got a gold crown and a sharp sickle—and does he ever know how to use it.

Most of us are so far away from farm life the only times we see sickles are on the flags of the communists and Muslims. But these curved blades didn't always mean a particular kind of government or religion; everyone used them to harvest their crops.

This Son of Man gets a message from the heavenly temple that it's time for him to reap because the earth is ripe to be harvested.

Then another angel comes out of the temple, gets told by the altar's fire-angel (how cool is that?) to harvest earth's grapes because they are quite ripe. When the clusters are cut off they get thrown into God's winepress of wrath and there is so much 'juice' that outside "the city" it's as high as a horse's bridles for almost 200 miles [300 km]. At this point, we don't know which city this is, but we're going to see the same picture of a bloody mess later and find out roughly where this lake of yuck will be.

So, putting these things together, one way to picture this vision is that the cloud-sitter is Jesus and he collects those who belong to him first. Am I sure about this? No, but we have two places where Jesus compared his people to a harvest. **Matthew 9:37–38** talks about those people who are ready to hear the gospel are like a ripe field that just needs workers to gather them in. **Matthew 13:23–30** talks about people as a crop ripening and having neighbor-weeds who are dangerous fakes. They all end up collected: the bad burned, the good crop in the farmer's barn.

The grape harvest is easier to puzzle out. The clusters are squished in God's wrath-press and real blood pools outside a real city. There are plenty of angels involved in the punishment of the wicked. The single angel harvester isn't a problem in a vision where a whole country is represented by one wild animal!

Revelation 15

Except for the seventh trumpet sounding back in 11:15, we haven't been pushing forward in the events of the great transfer of power from the Earth Dwellers to Jesus since chapter 9. Now it's time to build to the climax and get this thing done. This chapter sets up the scene much like chapter 5 did because once those bowls start tossing, all heaven breaks loose!

John uses a phrase we've seen a couple of times already, telling us he sees a great "sign" in heaven. The woman was one, her enemy the Dragon was next, then the Beast's prophet makes these signs, and we're going to see some "frogs" do them too. But this sign is one of the good ones—well at least for Jesus's people!

Seven angels have the seven final plagues. When they are done, it's going to be all over. God will have poured out every ounce of his wrath on the earth.

But John doesn't just notice these dangerous dudes, he next focuses on something we were told was going to happen in the last chapter. All those people who were assured that death was far better than submitting to the Beast? They did get killed, but look what's happened to them! It's been a long time since we saw that glassy 'ice rink,' and this time it's lit with fire. These martyrs may be using harps, but somehow I doubt they're using a stage lit up like that to present God with a lullaby concert.

John doesn't tell us what Moses' song is, but you can go back to **Exodus 15** for yourself and read it—I'll wait... Do those sound like wimpy lyrics? Oh, no. And the "Song of the Lamb"? God is great, almighty, just, true, king, fearful, glorious, holy. Every single nation will have no choice but to worship him because everyone can see he's judged anyone who refused to fear him.

Now that's going to be an epic worship event.

After some jamming with the martyred crowd, John looked at the "tabernacle of the testimony" up there in heaven and sees the inner sanctuary had been opened. That's when the angels of the last plagues come out dressed just like Jesus and are given bowls full of the last of God's wrath. And you can see how fierce God's anger is because even up in heaven the smoke of his glory and power is so great no one could go in until after everything is finished.

Revelation 16

It's go time.

But first, let's think about these bowls. In **Exodus 12:22** we first run into such containers. They were to hold the blood from the slaughtered lamb so the Israelites could dip their hyssop branches in and smear the blood on their doors, protecting their firstborn sons. Moses uses them as part of the sacrificial worship of God in **Exodus 24:4–6**. He sprinkles half the blood on the altar but saves half of it in bowls.

Later the tabernacle and temple were equipped with basins—big bowls—near the altar to sprinkle on the people and furniture. Yes, it's gross, but talk about making you take your promise to God seriously!

Now, these heavenly bowls aren't full of blood, but with God's wrath, and has he ever blown his top!

- Bowl #1: Disgusting and painful sores on every person with the Beast's mark or that even worshipped his image.
- Bowl #2: Entire ocean turned to old blood, killing every sea creature in it.
- Bowl #3: Rivers and water springs turned to blood.

Hmm, we're seeing blood a lot here, aren't we?

Do you see what happens in **verses 5–6**? Talk about cool. Here, when everything under his control gets messed up, we find out there's been an angel whose job is to be in charge of earth's freshwater sources! We don't worship such beings, but it is amazing to realize there are creatures a little like naiads for real.

And this water angel honors God, not for sparing his domain, but for punishing the Earth Dwellers who won't worship the eternal and righteous Creator who deserves it. And, the water angel knows when Jesus's people get martyred. Their blood seeps into the earth, and the angels of earth notice.

- Bowl #4: The sun becomes scorching hot

We finally get some reaction from the Earth Dwellers here, and what we see them doing makes for some of the saddest verses in the whole Bible. Instead of repenting and honoring God as the water angel did, they curse God and say horrible things about him—my guess would be saying God is evil to dare hurt them this way.

- Bowl #5: Throne of the Beast and his kingdom filled with darkness

It doesn't say anything here to tell us what would cause so much pain they chew up their tongues. But let's think about this for a minute. They've had terrible sores since Bowl #1, but the lights don't go out until Bowl #5. While this could be a thick darkness that can be felt like God sent on Egypt (**Exodus 10:22**), today we have electrical devices that could provide us with ways to see even in this kind of situation.

But what if God collapsed their electrical grid and made it so that even things that run on batteries just wouldn't work? What would happen to you if you had no radio, TV, game console, or any other device? If you're like most of us, you would have a little trouble finding anything else to do—even with a sunny day outside. Now it's pitch black everywhere with nothing to distract the Earth Dwellers from their pain and the knowledge of the God who is bringing these judgments on them.

This still doesn't convince them to repent; instead, they just keep talking trash about God.

- Bowl #6 Euphrates River dries up into a highway for eastern armies

Like the Seals and Trumpets, John's list takes a break before getting to the last bowl. And the Evil Frogs we see next don't come as a judgment from God. They are the messengers of the Anti-Trinity members. But, as we see all through history, the busier Satan gets trying to accomplish his own plans, the more God is at work behind the scenes.

These kings believe they're assembling to get rid of Jesus's power once and for all, but they don't realize it will actually end up being the "great day of God Almighty."

It's interesting to see John switch from what he was observing to quoting Jesus's words just for **verse 15**. Do you remember the other place Jesus announced he was coming as a "thief"? Matthew 24:43. What was his point there? That the guy in charge of the "house" wouldn't have let anyone steal his stuff if he knew when to be on guard. We also saw people who would look like good Christians to others, but be totally ashamed at Jesus's real return (Matthew 24:48–51).

It doesn't really matter who gathers all the armies of the world, but we do know those evil frogs were assigned this job by the Dragon & Co. so they can't know it's also God's plan to collect them.

You've probably heard about this place called Armageddon. We usually think of it as The End of the World, like the movies, but it's more like The Beginning. It's also a real place, usually called Megiddo or Jezreel, that you can visit in northern Israel. Since the time when there have been enough of Noah's descendants alive to have armies, this valley has been a place of warfare. For example, the ancient Egyptians could ride their chariots north only by passing through it.

• Bowl #7 Greatest earthquake of all time, and an epic hailstorm

We've heard from the altar in heaven, the Holy Place in the temple, and now a loud voice says, "It is done." This is it. The transfer of power is happening now. We'll be getting more details about what Jesus and his team do on earth later (much later), but this plague is the last of God's global judgments. Everything after this is just the mop-up crew.

Earthquakes are fascinating to geologists. We now know they occur when the giant plates of earth's crust snag and then slide past each other. But geologists who take the Bible's beginning at its word do not believe God created the world with regular earthquakes—that would hardly be part of a "very good" (Genesis 1:31) creation! They see the flood as the event that triggered the first massive earthquakes with the deep waters fountaining upward (Genesis 7:11), breaking apart these plates, and we have been experiencing the tension this caused ever since.

So, when it's time for Jesus to reign over the earth in person, it's hardly going to be a utopia if people are still regularly getting squashed by earthquakes. There have already been four earthquakes mentioned in Revelation (6:12; 8:5; 11:13,19), and this one is the final, unprecedented, global quake.

God never tells us straight out, but I believe this will be the last earthquake ever. All the tension around the Ring of Fire and every other fault line on earth will be released, never to build up again.

And just how massive will this quake be? Enough to divide the "great city" into pieces and knock all the cities on earth to the ground. Living in the age of the skyscraper, it is mind-blowing to think of Manhattan, Tokyo, and all the other massive downtowns flattened—all in a single hour. No wonder God doesn't have to do anything else afterward!

This isn't even the biggest effect the earthquake has: all earth's mountains are rearranged, whether they are islands swimming in the ocean or rise high above like the Himalayas. What this will do to earth's geography is something only God knows.

Now I want to show you some fascinating prophecies about Jerusalem. They still work if the meaning is just that "highest" equals "most important," but what if it's talking about the physical world too?

- **Isaiah 2:2** tells us the mountain of God's temple will be taller than any other mountain on earth.
- **Micah 4:1** says the place of God's temple, Jerusalem, will be the highest—chief—mountain.
- **Ezekiel 40:2** starts a vision he had of a future temple on a "very high mountain."

We will learn that the eternal New Jerusalem will have no temple, so these prophecies must be fulfilled before that time. Can you imagine the upheaval of the crust of the earth to lower Mount Everest and raise Jerusalem up higher than any of the mighty mountains we have today? Mind. Blown.

But wait, there's something coming for dessert: hail, weighing around 100 pounds [45 kg]. A hailstone the size of your two fists can knock a man out and damage a car. These will be 18" [45.5 cm] across—of solid ice.

Do the Earth Dwellers finally repent and admit God is the real Lord of earth, sky, and them? Oh, no, they only abuse his name and character even more because they are so angry he dared do this to them.

And now it's time for God to remember Babylon the great...

Revelation 17

So, if you grew up like me you first learned about this 'profession' of prostitution from the Bible. From early times God compared worshipping anything besides him to a wife who sells herself to other men for what they can offer her. It sure helps us picture just how horrible God feels when we worship anything else! This whole chapter is all about the greatest false worship system ever.

The angel invites John over to watch this last fake that has corrupted every ruler on earth get destroyed.

Whether the wilderness is important or has anything to do with the location of the other woman, Israel, we don't know. But the beast we can understand better. First, if she's riding it, she's in charge of the beast, not the other way around. This fake worship lady is directing and using the beast.

This Scarlet Beast has a lot of similarities to the one in chapter 13:1:

- Blasphemy
- Seven heads
- Ten horns

It seems clear this wicked woman is in control of the government of this last kingdom.

How sad it is to see such beautiful things as John mentions in **verse 4** being used for such evil, but this is what happens in the real world. Whether you read the Old Testament, visit a history museum, or travel the world, you will see such luxurious materials being used in the worship of false gods.

We don't see what she does with the cup, but the angel already told us what happens when a ruler drinks out of it. He becomes "drunk" with her wine. If you know anything about what too much alcohol does to someone's brain, you can see how powerful a picture this makes. People will destroy their lives to get more because it makes them feel so good, but it can transform kind people into monsters. Even the 'nicest' drunk can kill themselves and others driving a car, and a ruler is "driving" a whole country!

The woman offers a mixture of all kinds of things that turn God's stomach (this is what "abomination" means if your Bible uses that word). Instead of being holy—clean and set apart as special for God—her worship makes her followers revoltingly filthy. As you grow up, you will see just how true this is, but God is going to put an end to this horror!

Her forehead tells it all, but like the word "mystery" it sets us puzzles as well. We are only shown this woman here at her end, but her face tells us she is the "mother" of other false worship and all disgusting practices. This makes us wonder if this figure is like the Israel woman, as ancient as the first idolatry. Remember, the spiritual beings who crave the worship we are supposed to give God have been evil since the dawn of history. And most religions are designed to only let a few people really understand what it's all about, which makes them mysteries.

One thing is sure, among the wicked deeds this woman does, the one that makes her "drunk" too is when she gets a taste of murdering Jesus's people. These are her enemies, the "saints"—holy ones—who refuse to drink her potion.

John is blown away by all this. It's too much to take in, even for him.

Now the angel gives us a mini section inside an intermission. We get a description of the beast the woman rides and does he ever look familiar. Besides what we already know, a few details are added.

The beast "was, and is not" but will rise out of that bottomless pit where the locust horses were hanging out. Lots of people have tried to figure out what this means. It might be a kingdom that existed in the past and is brought back for the time of the end. The words used also remind us of what John says about God back in chapter 1. Only God was, is, and forever will be, but it's not surprising that the fake god pretends to be equally immortal.

And you can imagine the fun Bible scholars have with the "seven mountains." Many over the centuries have believed this was a symbol for Rome on its "seven hills." And there is no question lots of false religious practices and evil have been part of the organized church which has its headquarters in that city. But this beast isn't the religious power; it's being *used* by the fake religion. And false worship has happened all over the world in the past and even now.

Should we keep our eye on Rome to become a world political power before the end? Can't hurt to be on guard, but it is wise to watch for evil religious worship of a 'god' who isn't God all over the earth.

One of the weak points of making the Beast a "revived Roman Empire" is the seven kings. The mountains equal kings—the angel said so. So, until large chunks of land in Rome come alive and start bossing everyone around, this doesn't fit. By the time John was recording Jesus's revelation, Rome was already on its eleventh emperor. This Beast only has five in the past, not ten. The only way to get this to fit Rome is to say all of Revelation's history finished with the destruction of Jerusalem in 70 A.D.

I don't think anyone can really make sense of the order of kings in **verses 9–11** until it happens in the real world. And as if 5+1+1+1 isn't enough to try to understand, now we meet *ten* kings!

But these "horns" are a bit easier to make sense of. We've met them before in Daniel; they're the horns of 7:7 (and three of them had better watch their backs in 7:8). Here, John gives us some more details.

These guys get appointed by the Beast, but don't hold any power of their own; at least at first they are picked to rule before they are even assigned a jurisdiction to reign over! The "one hour" probably doesn't mean sixty minutes, but with the "little while" of verse 10 we get the idea this government is going to be really short-lived, especially for these ten rulers.

Like modern governments, the Beast has the Lawless One, the Antichrist, as its head, but then he appoints a kind of "cabinet" of these secondary rulers. And he is going to use them to fight Jesus, but they are not going to win!

Verse 14 includes a KEY for Jesus's army. We'll see more of what they do in chapter 19, but there we find almost no details of who, or even what, they are. Here we are told those with Jesus are "called and chosen and faithful." There is only one class of beings the Bible describes this way. 1 Peter 2:9 describes his readers chosen and called. Paul calls the church faithful in Colossians 1:2. While angels are also faithful, we never read about them being these three things like true Christians are.

Since we know the Beast government is going to cover the whole world, it's no surprise that the "waters" around the woman represent every group of people. It's sad to think how many will believe her lies, even when Jesus is making himself visible.

But that doesn't mean everything will go great for this Mystery Babylon. The government rulers "will hate" her. They may have gotten what they wanted from her wine, but they don't like worshipping her. And they sure don't like her to have so much wealth.

Here's another KEY to the Babylon of the future. Lots of Bible teachers mix chapters 17 and 18 together as if there was only one Babylon. But stop and think about this:

Who destroys this Mystery Babylon? Is it God's judgment? No, it isn't. The Beast's governmental leaders all hate her and they take everything she has and eat her themselves. They will absorb every part of this false religion into their government's power; and what they can't use, they burn up. We aren't told when or how this happens. I think it could be when the Lamb-Dragon talks the world into building the statue of the Beast-Antichrist and forces everyone to worship him. If you have an idea you think is better, let me know!

Part of why so many mix the next chapter in with this one is what we are reminded of in **verse 17**. God can work through the cruelest, most evil tools. He is in charge, even of these kings who cooperate with the Beast because it's all part of God's plan to pull the wicked together under one ruler.

Verse 18 throws one final puzzling piece out for us. The fake religion woman is a city. And not just any city but one that rules over the rulers. No wonder so many think this must mean Rome! When you read Medieval European history you run into the popes and kings butting heads often because the pope wanted to be over the kings and the kings wanted no such thing.

But if the city at the center of the false religion is the government's capital, why in the world would the kings destroy their own home? A thousand years ago the governments were all over the place but the pope still tried to run things from his small city-state. Wherever this religious center is, it's going to try to run the show—until the kings lose their tolerance for the tool that had used, and been used by, them.

Revelation 18

The first verse here is a good one to remember when you see angels presented as lovely young ladies—or worse, babies. Oh, no, the spiritual beings in charge of protecting us and doing whatever God asks of them are nothing like wimps!

As this angel lights up the planet with his glory, he makes a huge announce-ment. Babylon "has fallen" even though John is going to watch her destruction *afterward.* This is a lot like the last verse of chapter 6 where they say God's wrath "is come." In English we don't talk like this: announcing something happened in the past when the event is still in the future. But in Greek they could and did.

Interestingly, no one tries to say what the angel announces this time must have already happened when he declared it; they can see he only means that it's absolutely sure to happen But the same form back in Revelation 6:17 gets twisted around to point to the past by many people—only because if it points at the future it messes up their ideas.

The history of Babylon goes all the way back to the time of Noah. Most scholars believe the Tower of Babel was located there and Nimrod, the first tyrant, ruled over this city. It was the first home for man-centered thinking of all kinds after the global flood.

For those who believe all biblical prophecy was fulfilled in 70 AD, the "fall" of Babylon is something they have to assume is symbolic. While Daniel experienced one of the defeats of the city, it was such a surgical strike pretty much only the king died. Alexander the Great liked the city so much he ordered his soldiers not to damage it. Instead of being wiped out in a single day as John describes, historically the city slowly sank into decay and the sands finally covered the remains only after the Muslims conquered the area. Today the city of Hillah is built right next to the ancient ruins. Nothing about John's prophecy fits the history.

Also, remember how lots of people combine Mystery Babylon with Babylon the Great and think this Babylon is the Roman Catholic Church? They believe this center of evil and luxury will have to be the city of Rome. They reason that John used "Babylon" as code language to keep the manuscripts from being confiscated by the Romans. They cannot picture modern Iraq (where Nebuchadnezzar's Babylon is located) ever becoming the center of world commerce.

Could they be right that the city God fries is in Italy rather than Iraq? I doubt it, especially with what we see about this city in the Old Testament long before anyone would have needed to write the Bible in code. Why not assume God meant what he said?

When you read through the Bible, it is interesting to notice how often God not only judges a person, people, or city by destroying them, he goes on to point out how even their memory will rot. We all have a built-in desire to leave our mark on the world, and God spends a lot of time showing us how our choices will affect this legacy.

Here in Revelation 18 we find that Great Babylon makes everyone drunk with her wine like Mystery Babylon did. Not only are they sinning sexually with her, she makes them rich with her luxuries.

Verse 4 is one of the things Jesus tells us in Revelation that I have thought about over and over. It's small, but I believe a KEY to understanding not just the future but today: *Even in this place of massive wickedness, God has his people.*

We are often tempted to think every person who is part of a worldly or evil system must be evil themselves. But here is the worst of all possible situations and God sends a call to his people to flee. Never let yourself write off a whole group of people, not even those running a place of greed and lust like this city.

At the same time, at some point we will have to follow the angel out, like Lot and his family did in Genesis 19, or end up destroyed in God's judgment. There are some consequences that don't just happen to individuals, they catch everyone in the area. Our only hope is to flee.

The idea of a people's sins "piling to heaven" is a fascinating one. Like the analogy of a "cup of iniquity," God uses a physical picture for what is happening spiritually. We might picture a pile of filthy laundry never getting washed until it reaches the ceiling—and in this picture, it's only at that point that God blows his top and incinerates the heap.

Verses 6–8 remind us that God is truly just. We reap what we sow. And, as farmers know, we reap later, the same kind, and more than we sowed. The only hope any of us ever has of finding mercy is to ask God to hide us in Jesus, who took God's judgment into himself so we didn't have to bear it.

It is good to remember that when God allows evil to happen, it's not because he's too weak to stop it. He is more than strong enough to force these evil people to 'take their medicine' even when they're the greatest city on the planet.

There are a couple of places in the Old Testament where a city got cocky and thought no one could possibly mess with them. It may seem odd, but when you study history and look around you, self-talk among members of a group like this happens all the time. "We're the best." "We deserve special treatment." "No one can mess with us." It's a version of pride that can be hard to spot because everyone around is echoing it back at you.

The scene from **verses 9–19** is extraordinary. We never really find out what God does to set the city of Babylon ablaze—no fireball from heaven or earth fissure swallowing it—instead we zoom away to join the kings and ship captains. And even at a great distance, they can see the smoke rising.

So, how do they feel about God destroying this city? They are in shock and mourning.

This reaction alone tells me the Mystery Babylon of chapter 17 cannot be this city. Mystery Babylon was destroyed by these same kings to make them richer. This Babylon is mourned by them because they believe without her they will never be rich again.

Verses 11–13 remind me of something important when I really want to buy something. There is nothing wrong with any of these things existing. Some of them will be used in God's own city, and all of them were invented by God himself. But the love of them is a dangerous sin. And stop and think about that last item.

Here is a great modern city, but because of the worldview they follow, they are comfortable selling human beings to the highest bidder. Even in Christian countries which don't allow it legally today, there is a secret trade in human lives. In every place, some people are willing to use helpless people to make large amounts of money by selling them to evil people. This unashamed use of people as merchandise is enough for us to see why God wants the whole place wiped off the map.

Look at how often John mentions that Babylon the Great is destroyed in just "one hour." A lot of this chapter echoes Isaiah's prophecy about the city of Babylon in chapter 47. **Isaiah 47:9** adds that it happens in an "instant in one day." Today we easily forget how long it would take to lay siege to a city and break it up—the fall of Jerusalem to Nebuchadnezzar took over a year. Then, even when the army broke in, the destruction took time.

Here we're talking about a modern city with skyscrapers. Until the 20th Century, the world had never seen anything like this instant destruction—except from a natural disaster like the volcano destroying Pompeii.

Just in case we think the merchants and kings were exaggerating about how quickly Babylon fell, in **verse 21** we get to watch a mighty angel give us a demonstration of how violent it will be. Nowhere else in Jesus's revelation to John is he shown a comparison like this, so it seems like Jesus really wants us to get it—when Babylon falls it's going to be the equivalent of a city-sized boulder being hurled down into the water. Can you picture the mighty splash bursting up and out?

While God could use a miracle to destroy Babylon the Great, there are a number of unfulfilled prophecies about her destruction that tell us which people will be used as Gods' weapons. Let's start with **Jeremiah 51**.

It's a long chapter, but you see its echoes all through John's book. **Jeremiah**

51:8 tells us that Babylon will be destroyed "suddenly." In **verse 11** we see the Medes, who lived on the south end of the Caspian Sea, are the ones attacking and in **verses 27–28** they are joined by the peoples on the west side of the Caspian Sea.

Isaiah 13 has so much about the Day of the Lord we have already studied it. But did you notice who comes to destroy Babylon? **Verse 17** tells us that it's the Medes again.

There are more verses that talk about Babylon's destruction coming from the "north" if you want to study more about this for yourself. Next time you read through the Old Testament you can collect these references. Right now I want you to notice two more things.

Do you know where God allowed the people of northern Israel to get deported to? Look up **2 Kings 17:6** to find out. Today there's a city the world has to keep their eye on in this area of the Medes homeland: Tehran, the capital of Iran. I can't help wondering if someday a number of their men discover they are actually Jewish and decide they hold to a higher allegiance than the Beast.

If my guess about all this is right we've already seen something that looks like the effect of a giant rock being flung down into the ocean that people are afraid to get anywhere close to. You know I'm not interested in turning locust-horses into modern army tanks, but this city's destruction is predicted to be carried out by God's human agents, and today we know a nuclear explosion could totally give us the kind of scene John witnessed.

All these prophecies about the destruction of Babylon are particularly confusing because they are so often double-layer, near+far prophecies. Remember, Daniel survived the coup of Babylon and finished his life serving the king of the Medes. But when you line up things like Babylon's "sudden" destruction (which is predicted seven times in the Old Testament) and how no one is to ever live in it again, we can see there's plenty of room for a disaster to fall on a real, future Babylon.

To close the chapter, we turn to see what those in heaven think about this city getting what's coming to her. **Verse 20** tells us it's time for them to rejoice! Why? Because they like blasting people? Oh, no. This city brought destruction on her own head by murdering all kinds of Christians and innocent people.

God doesn't overlook the abuse or destruction of even the smallest life. He notices. There will be vengeance.

Revelation 19

We are almost done. All that remains of history is mopping up the bad guys and the grand celebration of God's people. And what a celebration! John gets pulled back to a heavenly focus by a vast crowd of voices giving great glory and praise to God. But this time it's not so much for his goodness as for his justice.

These people recognize they have been avenged, and guiltless people will never be harmed again because God has destroyed Babylon the Great. Beautiful as her city and stores had been, there had also been great evil and it was filled with the murder of many of God's servants. The souls under the altar are no longer crying out for vengeance. God has done it and everyone in heaven worships him—even for the eternal smoke of the burning city.

Have you ever heard the Hallelujah Chorus? **Verse 6** is where Handel got the words for his mighty anthem. And I have the feeling the heavenly version is going to be even more spectacular.

But this is far more than the most awesome music concert in history. It's the start of a great party; the "wedding of the Lamb" has come.

We won't get more about this "supper" or feast later, so I want you to look up one of the most incredible passages in the Bible, **Luke 12:36–38**. When Jesus comes back to those who watch for him, he's going to throw a feast, and...it's going to be uncomfortable at first, but can you imagine what this will be like? Wow!

A few times in my life I've heard a pastor brave enough to tackle the book of Revelation or at least this chapter. I'm glad they were doing what they could to help their people not be scared of the Bible's prophetic sections, but I wish they'd taken some more time to think about **verse 8**. The idea I heard was that the fine linen clothes these saints wear to the wedding are their own righteousness.

What does God tell us about our personal righteousness? Can I do good things to please God into giving me clothes? **Isaiah 64:6** has something to say about this idea. What about the thief who is promised paradise on the cross in Luke 23:42–43. And what about those who find Jesus at the end of their lives? Are they stuck wearing underwear forever?

In **Matthew 22**, Jesus tells one of his versions of the King and the Wedding Feast. This time he adds a disturbing but important detail in **verses 11–13**. One of the rag-tag guests they dragged in isn't wearing a "wedding garment." There were lots of people at the wedding who were beggars or outcasts. But only one guy gets tossed into "outer darkness" for not wearing the right clothes. This tells us there were clothes made available to these paupers; the problem with this guy is that he had refused to put a donated robe on.

John already told us about the clothing God's people are given back in chapters 6 and 7. Everyone is given a robe by God (6:11) and we clean them in Jesus's blood (7:14). No one gets into God's house any other way. No one is so good on her own she gets a super fancy dress with a train down the aisle. No one is so lowly he only has a loincloth on. Paul tells us in Romans 3:22–23 that all our righteousness comes from Jesus, not a bit from ourselves.

And here's the real point. Human beings are creatures. In the psalms, David wonders why God bothers to pay attention to us at all. But he does. And he doesn't just put up with us hanging around, he wants us near him, dressed in amazingly expensive, clean clothes—made of linen like the priests and fanciest people would wear.

Depending on what kind of church you attend, you might run into some interesting ideas about whom Jesus is marrying. John the Baptist was the first to compare Jesus's relationship with people to a bridegroom's in John 3:29. Jesus told a parable about a king throwing a wedding feast for his son in Matthew 22, and that his going away was like a king traveling from his home to marry a wife in Luke 12:36. And there are the ten young women with their lamps waiting for the bridegroom to start the party in Matthew 25:1–14.

In Ephesians 5:23–32 Paul compares "the church" to a wife and Jesus to the husband. So, many pastors teach that the church is the Bride of Christ. The Bible agrees—as long as they have the right definition of "church."

Many of these preachers believe there will be people in heaven who are *not* part of Jesus's bride. They don't think anyone who feared God before Jesus's crucifixion counts, and they also don't think anyone who turns to Jesus after he raptures his church is part of the Bride. Some go so far as to say those redeemed before Jesus's death are God the Father's bride since the prophets compared Israel to God's bride in places like Isaiah 54:5, Jeremiah 3:14, and Hosea 2:19.

But what if the word for "church"—*ekklesia*—is used of God's people in the Old Testament? Moses called the "church" together in Deuteronomy 4:10 to listen to him give his last sermon. David called the people of Israel the "church" when he faced Goliath in 1 Samuel 17:47 and talked about praising God among the "church" in Psalm 35:18. Even Job in 30:28, who wasn't an Israelite, sadly remembered how he cried out his complaint in the "church."

For those who believe the Father has his own bunch of people while Jesus has a different bunch, I have just one question: How does any human being gain enough righteousness to be worthy of heaven? Through Jesus's death on the cross. Did that change when Jesus died and rose again? Will this method change when Jesus announces his return with his glorious sign in the sky and gathering of his elect?

If the way into God's presence doesn't change, then why try to split the Trinity and the redeemed into groups based on time, when God is eternal unity?

OK, we've fried our brains with some ideas so complicated many seminary professors never unravel them. We can kind of understand why John falls down in **verse 10** to worship the angel who tells him these things. And the angel's response is an important one, in fact, it is a KEY idea in the Bible: if a being accepts worship, he is either evil—like demons or wicked men—or he is God made visible. And God made visible equals Jesus.

The last thing the angel tells John sounds a bit confusing, but he's reminding John to keep his focus on the real source of knowledge. The real Spirit of prophecy will always tell the truth about Jesus.

It's time for the final scene in the great war for the control of the earth and its people. We don't get all the story of Jesus's return to the surface of the planet here. A few scholars have taken the time to study all the little details the prophets gave us, like in Isaiah 63:1, and they can trace the full journey he makes to arrive at this last battle. But for now, we'll just look at where John tells us Jesus ends up fighting the last battle.

Because it's time for Jesus to switch from being the Lamb who allowed himself to be murdered to being the conquering Lion of Judah. He's not on a lowly donkey anymore; he's on a white charger. He is crowned with the power and the right to be king many times over. He does what he says, he allows no lie to stand, and he is absolutely right—even as he comes as the destroyer of the wicked.

You do not want him for your enemy.

We can only guess why Jesus wears a name we don't know. It does remind us of the secret name he gives us back in Revelation 2:17. But I like to think of it being a way to express that Jesus's existence doesn't come from outside of himself, like everything in creation. He is God. Of course God is going to have things about him we can't understand.

If you would like to wear blood-soaked clothes raise your hand! We're modern people, we know blood is gross, but that wasn't the way the ancients looked at it. We do know this isn't Jesus's own blood staining his robe because **Isaiah 63:3** tells us it happens when he destroys his enemies all by himself. Nothing can stop Jesus or make him sick, even having to wipe out an epic army of the wicked. Getting up close and personal with your enemy is going to spatter your clothes with their dying blood. And Jesus is going to deal with millions of these rebels.

Even though Jesus is more than able to wipe the wicked out all alone, he doesn't want to be lonely. He brings his people along to watch.

For years I wondered which beings would be following Jesus. I have zero desire to be part of any army, even one that is sure to win. I'd rather be a cheerleader from a safe distance—like bright, clean heaven. So I wanted to know: do human beings follow Jesus on this last great quest or are these angels?

First of all, I forgot to pay attention to the fact that these are "armies" plural, not just one group. So that alone tells us it's probably both humans and angels. Jesus tells us angels will for sure be there in Matthew 16:27 and Mark 8:38.

Both the Old and New Testaments call those who come with Jesus "saints," his "holy" or "set apart as separate and special" ones. Both **Zechariah 14:5** and **1 Thessalonians 3:13** say so, and **Psalm 149:9** says this is the honor or glory all his "saints" have.

We haven't talked about this word yet, but it's a KEY word, not just for the end but for all of the Bible. "Saint" means holy one and we find this name for holy people all over. While the angels who didn't rebel are "holy" (same word), all of God's people are called the "holy" from Exodus to Revelation.

Did you know the name "Christian" is only used in the Bible three times? "Believers" is used twice. But "saints" is used 61 times to describe Jesus's people, and over a dozen of those times are right here in Revelation. We are holy, even when it can be hard to tell at the moment.

Some people who want to divide Jesus's people into all different groups talk about the "Tribulation Saints" of Revelation as if they are some different class of Jesus's followers. But it's God's servants, the "saints" who attend the wedding feast in white robes in **verse 8** and get to accompany Jesus on his victory campaign.

Remember how one of the biggest claims of people who believe Jesus will rapture his church before anything else happens in Revelation is this: John doesn't use the word "church" after chapter 3 until the very end (22:16). They use this missing word to confirm what they already believe, that the "church"—in their mind Jesus's people only from the Day of Pentecost to the Rapture—isn't part of the events taking place on earth. But somehow they always forget to mention this would logically mean these people wouldn't get to be part of the wedding feast or join Jesus here, it's the "saints" who wear the wedding garments!

So, whether Jesus lets me skip out on this one or I'm good with coming along, **verse 14** tells us Jesus's armies get to ride on white horses. I have never ever read a book or heard a pastor talk about the stables, pastures, and paddocks of heaven, but there have to be a ton of them to provide mounts for all of us!

And if there are horses, are there dogs? cats? gerbils? We aren't told one way or another, but these horses tell us there are for-absolutely-sure animals, and that makes me happy.

I kind of wish everyone paused for a silent half-hour here like they did at the beginning of chapter 8. Jesus is about to use his voice as he never has before.

The name we are allowed to know Jesus is called here is, the "Word of God." At the dawn of creation he *said* things and creation popped into being. Even when Jesus was mortal he *spoke* and the raging storm instantly dropped, while waves that normally take hours to spend their energy turned smooth as glass (Mark 4:3). When Jesus *said* "I am" to the guards sent to arrest him, they were knocked backward. His word brought the dead back to life and sent the demons scurrying far away.

You've seen epic movies? Watched the bad guys or heroes end it all with one reverberating action? Jesus's word is unstoppable, unlimited power. He makes fantasy movies look like small trickery.

All the rebel kings of earth have gathered to stop Jesus from stealing their kingdoms from them. We saw this day coming several times back in the Old Testament.

Remember the way the flesh melts off the bad guys and their horses in Zechariah 14? Now we find out God's cleanup crew for the mess, all the carrion birds of the world. Eww!

The people gathered to fend off Jesus come from all levels of society from servants to kings. Reading **verse 18** in English I used to think "all" meant every single person on earth, but it just means "all sorts." While millions from everywhere on earth will never go back to their homes because of their rebellion, there will be scattered people left alive for Jesus to rule with his iron rod.

Right there, in person, is the leader of the rebellion, the Beast and his fake Lamb-Dragon Prophet. They don't get turned to goo. Instead, Jesus captures them and opens a portal straight into the eternal Lake of Fire and lava. It's going to be just the two of them in there for a long, long time.

But everyone with them, probably after watching their leaders dealt with so swiftly and effortlessly, is utterly doomed.

I think it might be a good idea to stay on Jesus's team, don't you?

Revelation 20

Did you know there were no chapter and verse breaks in the Bible until over a thousand years after John finished writing his book? The first six verses of this chapter tie right in with chapter 19.

As soon as Jesus finishes tossing the Beast and his Prophet into the Lake of Fire and melting away their entire army, an angel descends from heaven to deal with the original member of the unholy trinity. Satan is not God's equal, not even close. A single angel is strong enough to chain him up and lock him away in the bottomless pit.

Many views of prophecy turn this "thousand years" into a symbolic, or "spiritual," time. If everything John was prophesying was fulfilled in 70 AD except for turning over the kingdom to the Father, then this period of time has already lasted nearly two thousand years.

We do know things like the "ten days" of Revelation 2:10 *can* be symbolic (and even for those martyrs it could have lasted exactly that long), but there is nothing in Revelation 20 that makes us *have to* assume the "millennium" isn't an actual length of time.

If John's account of Jesus's earthly reign is merely spiritually showing how God's kingdom has been growing over the years, it could hardly be described as him using an "iron rod." There has been a whole lot of evil and lies allowed all these years, and they expect us to believe these tragedies have happened *without Satan to deceive us*? Well, they say his power is "limited," but do we really see it any more limited than it was before Jesus came to earth?

Why not let the Bible mean what it says. We've already seen the 7 and 3 and a half years enough times to expect them to be real. Why not this earthly reign?

Some people assume **verses 4–5** tell us the only people who have died and come back to life to reign with Jesus are those who get murdered for refusing to submit to the Beast. You can see why; they are the only ones John mentions here. But that's because we've already seen the rest alive again in Revelation 7. Does he *have to* mention them again to mean they're included?

Jesus told his disciples *they* would reign with him in **Matthew 19:28**. They weren't martyred under the Beast. Daniel 7:27 says the "saints" will rule. Paul tells the Corinthian church *they will all* be judges in **1 Corinthians 6:2–3**. In Romans 11:15 he makes the case that when the Jewish people all recognize Jesus as their Messiah the resurrection will happen.

Verse 5 tells us this is exactly what is happening. The "first" resurrection is the one when all those who feared God and are part of his kingdom come back to life. Most will already be alive when Jesus destroys his enemies and locks up Satan, but those who had been murdered between the time he gathers his elect and this day won't miss out on the fun!

The Reign of Jesus over the Mortal World

This time when Jesus and his people reign over the earth is one of the most exciting to discover in prophecy. We aren't given many details, but we are given enough to know this is going to be a time like no other in history. And it sounds like a lot of fun!

Paul does an amazing job pulling together what the Prophets foretold about this future time in **Romans 8:17–23**. Remember how Adam's sin turned over control of the world to Satan and *broke* everything? Jesus's return to reign in person is going to *fix* everything. And the entire universe is anxiously waiting for this time. But what will it look like?

Let's start with everyone's favorite, **Isaiah 11**. Read the whole chapter and you'll see:

- The animal kingdom is going to be vegetarian and harmless
- All kinds of nations will serve God
- There won't be any tension between people groups

The change in the animals reminds me of Mark 2:5–12 when Jesus asked the Pharisees and Bible copiers whether it was easier to restore a man's body or his relationship with God. He used the healing of a man's helpless body to show his power over his soul. In the future, Jesus is going to restore the animal kingdom to show how he can restore human kingdoms.

When God first invented animals and people he told every one of them, even the *T. rexs* and mosquitoes, that they were to eat plants (Genesis 1:30). When Jesus comes back he is going to reestablish his "very good" creation much as it was at the beginning.

Ezekiel 34:25 tells us it will be safe enough to sleep in Israel's woods. They won't need to fear bandits or wild animals. (We'll see more of this chapter when we get to the human government.) **Hosea 2:18** calls what Jesus does with the animals a "covenant."

Ezekiel gives us by far the biggest section on the future kingdom of Jesus we find in the whole Bible. From chapter 40 to the end, we have 8 chapters of what the temple, the property lines, the festivals, the offerings, and a bit of the life of Israel will be like when the kingdom is restored. And this is clearly not a normal restoration.

My favorite part is **Ezekiel 47**. He spends a whole chapter of the Bible discussing the river that flows out of the temple mount. Ezekiel doesn't tell us how it splits into two directions like **Zechariah 14:8** does. But nowhere else in Scripture do we find out the trees will be thick as it heads towards the (once) Salt Sea and how there will be bunches of fishermen along the banks.

A KEY to this time is to notice people still eat fish. **Luke 24:42** tells us Jesus ate fish after he got his resurrection body. Land animals are off the menu during Jesus's reign, but fish are still allowed.

I wonder whether the marshy areas of the Dead Sea get left salty so we can harvest the healthy salts from there as we do today? Whatever Ezekiel's prophecy points to, it is totally fascinating to think about.

Psalm 72 is a double prophecy, with both a near meaning about Solomon and a far one about the Messiah. One of the things David points out in **verse 16** is that under his reign there will be such rich crops growing in Israel the stalks will be like a great forest.

Lots of psalms point to the coming reign of Jesus over the whole earth. Two of the clearest are **Psalm 96 and 98** that mention how the trees, water, and hills rejoice to have God reigning over them.

Habakkuk 2:14 talks about how the whole earth will know God's glory, just like the sea is covered in water.

Isaiah 2 tells the story of God taking over the earth in backwards order. We already talked about verse 2 and Mount Zion getting physically raised up. Now be sure to notice **verse 4** where the people take their old weapons and turn them into gardening and farming tools. They'll still use sharp things, not to hurt people but to grow food.

Micah 4:1–9 starts out almost the same as Isaiah 2. It adds that everyone will be able to live at peace on their own property growing grapevines and fruit trees.

Isaiah 65:17–25 is one of the longer prophecies about the millennium. It starts out sounding like it will be the way things stay forever. It's one of the few places where the double prophecy is all in our future. Some of this looks like the Eternal State, which we'll learn more about soon in Revelation. But does all of this prophecy fit the life that goes on without changing forever?

Verses 20–22 give us a fascinating KEY to life during this time. Ordinary people are going to live long lives in peace, but they will be *mortal* lives. Babies will be born and not die, and if a person dies around their 100th birthday, everyone will assume they are rotten sinners. Most people will live about as long as a tree does, and most trees live between 100–500 years.

Long ago we had people who lived to these kinds of ages. If you read the beginning of Genesis (chapter 5) you'll see Adam and those born before the flood of Noah's day lived nearly a millennium. Job (42:16) lived 140 years after his traumatic experiences, and even Abraham lived to 175 (Genesis 25:7).

Jesus tells us in **Matthew 22:30** that those of us with resurrection (or raptured) bodies don't get married. We won't be having children during this time. And we sure won't be dying, not even after living for centuries. All these people in Isaiah's prophecy are still mortals. All the babies will have a choice whether they want to belong to Jesus or not—and we'll see more about what happens to them at the last end of history.

Israel during Jesus's Reign

Back in Daniel 9:27, we were told the prince who was coming would make a "covenant" with "many," but halfway through the seven years, he would force them to stop sacrificing and bring the "abomination of desolation" instead.

Ever since the Jewish people as a whole (there have always been some who didn't) missed Jesus's first coming, they have rejected the idea that he is the real Messiah. But someday this is going to change.

Zechariah 12 is all about Israel's role in future events. The nations are going to hate her and gather to fight her, but God will strengthen all of Israel and do mighty things with the people of Jerusalem. The most exciting thing is what he tells us in **verses 10–14**. Finally, finally! Every Israeli left alive will recognize they had pierced their own Savior and will mourn for what their ancestors did to Jesus.

It is sad to learn what it will take for them to get to this point. **Zechariah 13** starts out talking about how the people will finally be truly clean and reject idols and lies, but then in **verses 8–9** we learn only one out of three Jews will have survived to follow Jesus. We don't know how many of the ones killed fell to the Beast's sword for refusing to cooperate with him. The Jews can be amazingly stubborn, so I'm sure there will be some who resist, but we also know the Two Witnesses spend three and a half years in Jerusalem and still have many Jews who reject them. So, some of those who die are sure to be people God brings his judgment on.

But at the end, can you imagine Jesus's joy when millions of his closest family all honor him as Lord and join his army? In fact, Paul tells us in **Romans 11** how God has allowed his Jewish people to reject him somehow to allow the rest of the world to find Jesus. But he reminds us in **verse 15** that when God brings them all back through Jesus it will be time for the resurrection from the dead.

Jesus isn't the only king in the future

Israel

Ezekiel 37:15–28 describes a time when the two kingdoms of Israel will be a rejoined and have a single king over them, "David." Many people think Ezekiel was really talking about Jesus, while some think it's the resurrected David himself.

Here are some things to think about with this "David" figure. In Ezekiel 46:16–18, we are told about the property rights of the Israelis in the future. The "prince" is given a good-sized chunk of land near the temple (see chapter 45), but he is not allowed to take any other land. He can only give his sons an inheritance out of the property he already owns. This prince worships God at the temple and leads the people in sacrifices both for them and for himself in chapter 45.

Whoever he is, it cannot be Jesus since he doesn't have sons (besides all of us spiritually) and he would never need to offer a cow for himself.

Even making this a resurrected David is difficult since he can decide to give his kids an inheritance if he feels like it. And why is David still offering sin offerings for himself thousands of years after his mortal life ends?

For me, it's easier to see this as a triple prophecy. Will Jesus be king at this point? Oh, yes, but he'll be over the whole world, not just Israel. And will David be there reigning with Jesus? Absolutely. But there's nothing stopping one of his descendants from becoming the mortal, reigning ruler of the nation and having children during this time. We know there are still men who can trace their family back to David alive today.

So, Israel has a real king and a real temple. What about everyone else?

The Nations during Jesus's Reign

We already looked at a taste of Jesus's rod-of-iron rule over the nations in **Zechariah 14**. Any kingdom that boycotts the worship festivals at Jerusalem gets zero rainwater for their crops for the next year. Even a developed nation is going to suffer greatly when its plants all start to wither and it can't grow any of its own food.

Are you surprised there are separate nations at all during this time? God likes people groups. Remember, he made sure to collect members of every single one for himself in Revelation 5:9. Daniel was told the other beasts he saw would have their lives prolonged even after their power was broken in 7:12.

Way back in Genesis God promised Abraham over and over (18:18, 22:18, 26:4) that all nations would be blessed through him. We know this is talking about Jesus rescuing us from sin and hell, but like everything, there is more than one layer to how God is going to work this out.

Isaiah 2 and **Micah 4** both open with non-Jewish people urging each other to come with them to worship in God's mountain. **Zechariah 8:18–23** has a rather fun prediction about the solemn holy days being turned into joyful feasts in Israel and bunches of people from other nations grabbing a Jewish guy's robes and begging to come with him to worship his God. I bet this will be something that happens right at the beginning of Jesus's reign as people are going from under the Beast's evil kingdom to suddenly being under God himself.

Isaiah 66:15–24 is the very end of that prophet's beautiful book (scholars tell us it's the loveliest in Hebrew) and it wraps up with another reminder of how God is going to finish off history. All the bad guys will be swept away and people from far away will tell others about his glory. The Israelis will be gathered like a tithe from everywhere to help the rest of the world worship.

But look at how unexpected and manly the very last verse of the book is. Somehow, the remains of the evil people will be visible for people to see their burning. This could even be a double prophecy where there is a smoldering burial place during the millennium as well as a portal window (no one can get through in either direction) to watch the eternal destruction of those who hated God.

The shortest chapter in the Bible will be perfect for this time in history. **Psalm 117** is only two verses long but it invites every person on earth to join in the praise to God for his loving-care to all of us and for his truth.

The End of History: Revelation 20:7-15

This section of prophecy isn't talked about much anywhere else in the Bible. The names John gives us in **verse 8** tell us to check out the one other place this event is predicted. "Gog and Magog" are the main-character nations leading great armies against God's people in **Ezekiel 38–39**. This could easily be a double prophecy since, starting in Ezekiel 39:9, we read about how disgusting and hard it is to clean up the mess after the battle. But for the immortal people who witness both attacks, I bet it's going to feel the same as they watch the enemy soldiers gathering to overthrow Jesus's rule.

John only gives us a handful of verses about this last event in human history, but there's a lot we can learn from them. Jesus and his administration have been in power for a full *thousand* years. During this whole time, everyone will be forced to live God's way with justice, honesty, and mercy. But kids who grow up in good homes with good neighbors, good weather, good religion, and good education are still Adam's descendants.

When Satan is allowed out to spread his lies again, people will listen—just like Eve did. In fact, under the most perfect conditions the world has ever seen, a vast army from across the globe is going to conspire to overthrow their "tyrant" master, Jesus.

Don't let anyone convince you we just need better nutrition, education, or government and then all our problems will go away. No one has to teach a toddler to lie, steal, and hit. We all are born sick with sin.

God doesn't have any grandchildren. Some people have parents who love Jesus more than anything in the world, but that doesn't mean their kids will. Each of us chooses or rejects Jesus for ourselves. Not even all the saints in history can convince us if we don't want to listen.

In many ways, Revelation 20 is the saddest chapter in the Bible. At some point, the only thing left to do with the bad guys is wipe them out.

Jesus and his people gather into one "camp" at the Holy City, Jerusalem. But then it's time for God the Father to take over. If you remember, Paul is the one who hints at what happens when the only thing left for the rebels is fire. 1 Corinthians 15:23–28 talks about this and tells us when the time comes,

Jesus will turn his authority over to his father so he can be "all in all."

We belong to Jesus because he is the one who paid for us, but he redeemed us "back to God" because that's what the Father wanted. Jesus isn't higher than God the Father, he himself is protected and led by him.

So, is it a smart thing to rebel against God? The people of Noah's day could have told these armies how foolish it is. And King David, the great prophet, tells us in **Psalm 58:9** how quickly this judgment will fall. Thorn branches catch fire quickly and burn hot, so, for the wicked to be gone even faster tells us they are fried in a matter of seconds.

Satan is a spirit being. A fire couldn't kill him, so he gets thrown straight into the eternal Lake of Fire where the Beast and False Prophet have been tormented for a thousand years already.

And that's the end of history. No more babies, no more battles, no more kings, no new person joining God's family forever.

The only thing left besides the Eternal State is the Final Judgment where the evil 'trinity' is about to get a lot of miserable company.

God's judgment is so terrifying the whole of creation runs away and vanishes. Everything to do with the world as we now know it will be gone, just like that. Some people believe God will recycle the existing material of creation into his forever home, but this verse tells us everything physical about the universe flees away. What God builds the New Heaven and Earth out of is not the same stuff we see today. Not even the same elemental molecules.

And it's time for every person who has ever lived to face God's decision for their fate. Even if they never admitted God was even real during their mortal lifetime, they are going to have to admit he is the Master.

Philippians 2:9–11 tells us that everyone, without exception, is going to bow and declare God the Father has made Jesus their Lord. While the verses don't say for sure that spiritual beings will be here, we know the demons are there from places like **Matthew 8:29**. 2 Peter 2:4 adds that some of the demons—perhaps like the locust army—were so evil they have already been bound in "chains of darkness" waiting for this day.

Now, here's a mind-blowing thought for us. Paul tells off the church at Corinth for taking each other to court instead of handling such things themselves. In **1 Corinthians 6:3** he makes an amazing statement, "Don't you realize we're going to judge angels?" Umm, no, we didn't, but—wow. By ourselves, we are far less powerful, but God has set his love on us. And talk about embarrassing for the demons to be bossed around by human pipsqueaks.

How are people judged on that day? There are three "books" used as evidence. Two are records of works and the other is the one that really matters, the Book of Life.

If you've ever seen people do things that were unfair and felt helpless to do anything about it—if you've ever heard of how people in history "got away" with being cruel to those under their power—you don't need to worry about them escaping God. They will face justice. And the punishment for everyone will fit their crime. Except for those who have asked Jesus to hide them under his sacrifice.

Those who have their names written in the Book of Life are spared "The Second Death" and will get to experience the wonders coming next.

- Moses knew about this book back in **Exodus 32:32–33**. He was willing to have his own name smudged out so God couldn't read it rather than have his people destroyed.
- David asked God to smear the name of the wicked out of this book in **Psalm 69:28**.
- Jesus told his disciples having your name written in heaven is the real thing to rejoice about in **Luke 10:20**.
- Paul asks the Philippian Christians to help everyone whose names were in this book in **Philippians 4:3**.

At least since the time of the ancient Egyptians, we've believed in an afterlife decided by our goodness. None of us can be good enough on our own to earn heaven, but there is no question the suffering of those who refuse Jesus will depend on how much they instead chose wicked selfishness.

Verse 13 is fascinating but scary to think about. All the people who had already been in torment will be brought out just long enough to see how evil they had been. Even those who died before the book of Genesis was finished, those who had been drowned in the flood, will still face their own choice to constantly think evil (Genesis 6:5).

But it won't get any better for them, because they are immediately thrown into the eternal Lake of Fire.

It doesn't matter how harmless a life a person lived. If they don't belong to Jesus, if he doesn't have their name in his book, they're done for. But this doesn't mean everyone is tormented the same way. God tells us very little about the levels of misery those who die the Second Death experience, but he does tell us enough to know it is fair.

Isaiah 14:4–20 is a double picture of both the king of Babylon and Lucifer himself. It's not an ordinary picture either; it is all set in the place of the dead. Everyone down there will consider this creature who destroyed so many and now doesn't even have a grave.

Ezekiel 28:1–19 is a similar double passage about a king and Satan himself. When you read the first part it sure sounds like what we've seen Babylon the Great claiming about herself, but this shows us the "anointing cherub" himself who had once been in Eden being thrown down for the kings to stare at. The Lake of Fire won't be fun for anyone, but it's going to equal humiliations unending for the totally powerless Satan.

Even people groups will face different kinds of judgment at this point. Jesus told the cities of Israel they would face worse punishment someday than Sodom and Nineveh because they rejected him in **Matthew 11:20–24**. He couldn't have been just talking about their destruction by an army because he mentions Sodom will be there on the future "day of judgment" even though it had been burnt almost 2,000 years before.

Each person will be judged based on the amount of truth they had been given. Those who had met Jesus would face far worse consequences for rejecting him than those who had no clue about him.

This is a good point to pause and wonder about the people who never had a chance to understand enough or learn enough to make a choice for Jesus or not. The final answer is that God didn't tell us how he decides these things, but we are given some good ideas.

- Jesus says children have guardian angels in Matthew 18:10
- King David the prophet expected to rejoin his son in the afterlife in 2 Samuel 12:23
- Moses and David asked God to *cover over* names in the Book of Life

If a name is removed from the book by inking over it, this means it had to be there at first. Small children and anyone whose brain doesn't work well enough to understand who Jesus is, would not be doing anything that would get their name blotted out by sin.

How this works out for people who lived in places where they never had a chance to hear about Jesus we'll have to leave up to him. But if you have a chance to tell someone, that job is on you. Jesus commanded us to pray for people to go out into the harvest field to gather people while there is still time. And God warned Ezekiel (and us) that if he didn't give a warning to those in rebellion, God would hold him responsible (Ezekiel 3:18–21, 33:8–9).

Whew, that was rough. But this is the end of any kind of death, suffering, and sorrow. Now it's time to catch a glimpse of the Eternal State!

Revelation 21

Psalm 102:26 tells us why God decided to make a new heaven and earth. Way back at the beginning of history the world had been "very good," but it didn't stay that way. In only a blink of an eye, Adam and Eve had rebelled and God had to pull down a series of punishments on both them and their kingdom. Even with Jesus to take care of it someday, the old earth was just that—old.

Why God doesn't create any seas again we can only guess; it will certainly give us more room to spread out but is sure to mean the weather is radically different. Symbolically, the "sea" is where the dragon and beast came out of earlier in this book, and the Mystery Babylon woman was on lots of water. Jesus's disciples had faced their scariest times following him around Israel while they were on a sea. For anyone who traveled by water, the sea was a terrifying place of separation from people and safety.

I'm sure there will be plenty of amazing views in the future that allow us to enjoy an experience like we have when looking at an endless watery horizon, but God decided there was no need for these reminders of the first judgment he brought on sin in his eternal kingdom.

It's been a while since we were aware of John being our guide, but in **verse 2** he tells us about watching the New Jerusalem coming down from heaven. And the city is as beautiful as a bride.

I have seen some claim that because the city is "coming" out of heaven it will forever be in orbit above the earth. After all, the moon is technically always falling towards the earth to stay in its circuit around us. But this is one verse, one possible witness, with a whole idea built on using "coming" instead of "came" or "dropping." If John had seen the city in the sky like a moon, he could have easily said so, but to him it looked like it was coming down from heaven.

Why have it descend from God at all? Why not have him build it up like a mushroom from the earth? This is Revelation, and we know that what things look like, do, and where they come from tell us important things about what they mean.

There has been a town called Jerusalem a little east of the Mediterranean since Noah was still alive. Abraham gave gifts to the priest-king of that town in Genesis 14:18–20. A lot of good things happened there, but a lot of evil did too. Idol worship and sinful practices were ritualized in all the streets. Jesus was condemned to death and marched through the streets to die just up the hill from the temple. Rome was allowed to slaughter around a million Jews there in 70 A.D. It was a place of blood and painful memories.

The New Jerusalem is God's own special creation, never touched by sin or any evil. Prepared, like Jesus told us he would, in the Father's house (John 14:2–3).

Verse 3 tells us the most incredible thing of all about the Eternal State. God won't be off somewhere special. He won't need to have sacrifices and offerings, or even prayers, to open a connection between us and him. He will be our next-door neighbor. Yes, he'll still be our God, but he'll be as close as our family is to us today. He will dwell—live—with us.

And God will set everything right. I've often imagined what God's handkerchief will be like. He's going to need some massive moisture-absorbing power to clean up all the tears I've shed, and, God's people have faced some horrific sadness. I don't know how it will work when we realize people we had hoped to spend eternity with, never really decided to join Jesus. I know it's going to make me cry for a while, but even that pain will be wiped away as God comforts me.

As a grown-up, I've learned about what happens to us when we go through a terrible time. We develop something called PTSD, where things can trigger our old pain and pull us right back into that memory as if it's still happening. God's tear-removal process is going to be so thorough, even the most traumatized of his children is going to never face PTSD again. We won't even accidentally hurt ourselves anymore!

Remember how in 1 Corinthians 15:26 Paul told us the "last enemy" was death? We have now seen it got thrown into the Lake of Fire. Death can't touch anyone who belongs to God ever again. We won't have to say goodbye, we won't even have the jolt of a vacation time that's over and we have to pack up and head far away from our loved ones.

God still has a throne to sit on in **verse 5**. He is still our master and we will still serve him, but it will be all joy and peace, our bodies and minds will be happy to cooperate with his commands.

Today, when we see bad stuff happening and there's nothing to do to stop it, **verse 6** sure helps keep things in perspective. Even when the whole earth was full of people trying to stop God, they couldn't do it. He is Creator; he is Redeemer. If God decides to do something, the beings he created can't change it. And that is very, very good for those of us who let him be our Protector.

A water-fountain of life is such a great picture of having our needs met. Jesus used this water to help the woman at the well in John 4 realize she needed something much deeper than well water. All of us have been so thirsty we can't think about anything else until we get a drink. And God is the one who can fill our needs—without us having to pay him a cent.

All over the Bible we have hints of the promised rewards God has for those who honor him. **Verse 7** tells us how amazing this promise is in just a few words; you might want to memorize it. We get *everything* and get to be called his child forever. Anyone whose name is in the Book of Life is a prince or princess—a child of the king. Wouldn't that be fun to call each other at church now?

Don't let **verse 8** make you think this promise of reward isn't for you. None of us gets into heaven by never getting scared. This verse is warning the people who love things in this life more than they love God. When it's time to either take the Mark of the Beast or lose your head, there will be people so scared they submit to evil. Others refuse to believe Jesus is real, and many more love their sin too much to let it go.

If you know your only way into heaven is Jesus, and you want to follow him with all you are, no matter what happens, verse 8 is not talking about you. It is reminding us we won't have any bullies, trolls, or other evil people with us. Everyone in all of the Eternal State is going to love God with all their being and none of us will ever sin again.

At last, it's time to look at our forever home; where everyone who belongs to Jesus and gets to live with God for eternity has a place.

We've already thought about how many people believe only some people in heaven get to be part of Jesus's bride. But at this point in Revelation there are no new people being added to the kingdom. There will never be another baby born (Luke 20:34–36), and no one can ever again choose to repent from their sin and turn to God. Either you already belong to God or you are in the Lake of Fire for eternity.

And what does the angel tell John this city represents? "The bride, the Lamb's wife." Every person, from Adam and Eve's son Abel (the first human being to ever die) to the last mortal to choose Jesus over their own way, is part of the "Bride of Christ."

We already talked about the idea of the city being in orbit since John sees it descending. Let's look at the other details he is given as he watches with the angel.

Do you remember someone else taking a person to a high mountain and showing him a great kingdom? Long before, Satan had tempted Jesus to take an evil shortcut to reach this point (Matthew 4:8), but Jesus knew better than to take an easy way out. This city with all its redeemed inhabitants was what he was willing to go through all his suffering in order to purchase forever!

We are given only a few verses about what our forever home will be like; every detail matters, so let's look at them. John tells us there is at least one really tall mountain within sight of the capital city. Personally, I hope we can enjoy snow sports up there with Jesus—but that's just a guess.

John spends the rest of the chapter absorbed with how amazing the city of God-with-us is. And the first thing he notices is how bright it is with God's glory. Remember how God the Father looked like jasper in 4:3? Now his whole city glows with the same kind of light!

Why have a wall and gates when you will never need to protect yourself from an enemy? The same reason a home on a tropical island has walls and doors. To mark where "home" starts and stops. There will be lots of adventures for God and his people, but home is where the walls are.

And, the gates, as well as the foundations, give God a chance to highlight some of his most honored people. Why pick the 12 guys the people of Israel are named after? Because God can work through even the most disastrous lives and transform them into something good. And, he had promised Jacob he would bless the whole world through his family (**Genesis 28:13–14**).

Jesus's 12 apostles weren't that much better a bunch than the sons of Jacob. Even after the Holy Spirit gave them far more power to do the right thing than anyone in the Old Testament ever had, they still could be fearful and have trouble with healthy relationships.

But just a minute! The 12 disciples of Jesus didn't all make it to this point. Judah of Issachar betrayed and rejected Jesus. So who is the last one with his name on the foundation? Acts 1 talks about the disciples having God choose one of two guys who had hung out with them throughout Jesus's ministry and the name of Matthias was picked. But we never hear a word about him after this point; there's no way he gets his name on a foundation row of heaven. **1 Corinthians 15:8–9** give us the answer. Jesus picked Paul to be his last apostle—like a baby who was born way overdue.

God never breaks his promises, even after the end of history.

Remember how we've looked at what people actually do in heaven besides lounge around on fluffy clouds? **Verse 13** tells us something rather surprising if we were picturing a vague, 'spiritual' existence. There are compass directions even in the Eternal State. How we know which way is north, John doesn't tell us, but we will know which way we're facing as we enter and leave the city.

Right after this, we get more every-day, normal stuff for such a sublime place. The angel showing John around is measuring things so we can know how big it is. But unlike the tape measure you or your dad has, this guy's rod is made out of gold!

And this city measures the weirdest of any we have ever heard of. It's a giant cube. Or, at least at one point, the length, width, and height are equal—the easiest kind of volume space to measure. If your translation gives some fancy measurement, here's the modern version: 1,380 miles [2,220 km] on a side.

Now, to compare this with something we know, the moon has a diameter of 2,159 miles [3,474 km]. I have never, ever heard someone talk about what a city of this size stuck on the crust of the planet must mean for the size and possible rotation of the New Earth, but however this works out it's a truly massive space.

No wonder God longs to fill his home with lots of people. There's room for everyone who was ever conceived to live in this place!

I'll let you look up what colors the foundations of the city are, but there is something cool to keep in mind. Back in **Exodus 28:17–20,** it lists the precious stones they were to use making the "breastpiece of judgment" for the high priest to wear. The names don't look the same in our Bibles because our English version was translated from Greek in Revelation and Hebrew in Exodus, but many people believe these are the same types of stones. In the Old Testament, the names carved on the stones were of the 12 tribes of Israel. In the New Jerusalem, they are marked with the 12 apostles.

We are all there, all together, for all eternity, as one united family.

Making the gates out of pearl has always felt special to me. Remember how a pearl forms? Something uncomfortable or even dangerous gets into an oyster's shell. The oyster can't get it out, but it can coat it with the *nacre* it makes to keep its home smooth and cozy. As this happens over the years, the foreign object becomes lost in the heart of something so beautiful Jesus used it in one of his parables (**Matthew 13:45–46**).

Redeeming us cost God more than anything: Jesus's own life. Choosing God costs us everything, even our lives.

The next little detail is something you've probably already heard about. Instead of having roads of tar, cement, brick, stone, or dirt, this city has a road made from gold. And not just any Fort Knox-variety gold, this is gold so pure you can see through it.

Why does this matter? First, God is rich. He can make anything he wants and he is generous. He didn't keep his gold for his throne and leave us to our poverty—everything he has is ours to share. And remember how Jesus warned us not to bother trying to hoard treasure on earth where things get broken or stolen? Here's why. Anything I might treasure on earth looks rather silly next to the true wealth my Father has to share with me!

I love the end of this chapter so much!

Verse 22 is one of the sweetest in the Bible. Remember how Adam and Eve would talk to God when the wind blew in the Garden of Eden? God would come for a while and visit with them. Now we have something even better, God lives with us. There isn't any need for a special place to seek for him; he is there, hanging out with us wherever we are.

At the same time, God hasn't stopped being spectacular. God's "Shekinah" glory and Jesus the Lamb are so bright we don't need anything else to light up the place like the noonday sun. **Verse 23** *could* mean there is no sun or moon in the Eternal State, or, it could mean the city shines whether the sun and moon are shining on them at any given moment or not. And with all that light, there's no need to close the gates, there is never a dark shadow for evil to try to slip in, even if it could get that far.

Before we wrap things up it's time to slow down for a KEY to the future very few people think about: the nations will bring their "glory and honor" into this new city. The things that are praiseworthy and valuable about each people from earth won't be gone. Somehow, the people who were part of a nation in their first life will be able to bring the best of their culture with them into the new world. Whatever your country and ethnic background may be, God likes it. You will still be recognizable as part of these groups even in the

Eternal State. So, look for me in the American section and hanging out with the Celtic musicians, and I'll look for you with whatever makes your culture special to God!

If you've ever been to a park or festival that celebrates some other culture, you have an idea of what this might look like. I know I could easily spend a few million years enjoying the best food, architecture, stories, and music of other times and places around the world. Sound like fun?

What's best is, what places like Disney and other experiences try to do, God will make sure is always true. There will be nothing—absolutely nothing—yucky, warped, or false about anything in this city. No mafia, no underbelly, no domestic violence, or even "white-collar crimes" like politicians and business leaders are infamous for today. Only people who belong to Jesus ever get in.

And remember what we learned in 1 John 3:2? When we see Jesus, we will be like him, not only with a new immortal body, but also with his way of thinking, loving, and choosing. No more sin nature, no more temptation, no more selfishness. It's going to make the best experience we ever had on earth seem faint and pale in comparison.

Revelation 22

The beginning of this chapter flows right along after the last one and doesn't change scenes until verse 6. In Genesis 2:10–14, we are told more about the river that split into four branches in the Garden of Eden than any other feature of our first home long ago. In Ezekiel 47 he got to cross the stream flowing out of the future temple until it became a river too deep to ford, and then he turned his focus to the healing trees along its banks. God likes rivers a lot; so much so that he has one flowing right out of his royal throne forever.

This river doesn't just have clean water; it has life-water, so whoever drinks it will never die. And it's so important it gets to flow right down the most important street in the eternal city. John doesn't mention seeing them, but maybe we can visit the center of the Capital by traveling with a kayak or gondola!

Ever thought about what we'll eat in heaven? God packs so much information into **verse 2** it is a KEY to what the whole Eternal State will be like.

First, there's the tree. It might be a gigantic tree like you might see in the mountains of California or at an amusement park, but God's already made some plants on this earth that are still a 'tree' without having a massive trunk. Aspens, sumac, banyans, bayberry, and other trees can spread not only from seeds but by growing new trunks from their spreading roots. Even hazelnuts can form a grove of interconnected trees that are essentially a single, giant organism.

The Tree of Life is far more special than anything we see in the world today, not only because of its location but what it can do. It is a "Fruit of the Month" tree, producing a new crop of tasty, healthy food twelve times a year. It's fun to imagine whether we will recognize each kind of fruit when we get there, but that's not nearly as important as what twelve months that circle round and round tell us.

Remember how some preachers will use the words of the angel in chapter 10:6 to claim there is no time in heaven? This tree tells us this idea is totally off from reality. Not only will there be time, there will be *years*. Because as soon as the Tree of Life bears the same kind of fruit it did twelve months ago, it's been what we call a year. Even the basic unit of time now connected with the moon will still be there. It's not going to bear 29 fruits to give us 29 months; it's going to still be 12 in a cycle, just like today. Time is going to flow much like it does now—just we'll never get old or run out of fresh, healthy, new time!

And the Tree of Life is a part of our eternal health directly. Its leaves heal "the nations." This reminds us, like we just saw, that people will still belong to their own people groups and countries. The Greek word for healing is the same one we get our word "therapy" from. We still use leaves for teas, oils, and skin lotions to heal our bodies today. Jesus is the one who heals our souls, but he is also the one who invented herbs and healing waters.

Now, what does all this mean about the Eternal State? It will be a physical one where time flows as we experience it now and we eat, drink, and have spa treatments.

Do you remember what the curse was that **verse 3** says won't make it into the New Jerusalem? When Adam and Eve rebelled against God's command and ate what he told them not to, God cursed the ground to make it produce thorns and prickles—plants that would hurt the people and animals that needed them for food. Eve was told her relationships would cause her great distress and God also cursed the serpent. Later, in the Law, God gave several commands that involved curses for evil behavior. You can see a terrifying list in **Deuteronomy 27:15–26**.

In the Eternal State, the ground will be completely free from the pain of sin, just like Paul told us would happen someday in Romans 8:21. And no human being or angel will ever do a single thing that would cause God to have to bring a curse on them. We will all be truly free.

We've already seen that God will live with his people before. Now we are reminded that he is still the boss, and you cannot separate the Father from Jesus, the Lamb who sacrificed himself to redeem us. God is always three, but he is never divided. To know and love one person of the Trinity is to know and love the rest. But, it's not surprising we don't see the Holy Spirit on the throne since he is, well, an invisible spirit who would rather we thought about the other two than focus on him.

And look at the end of the verse. Not only does God get to make the rules, we are going to be working for him—forever. Whatever our life looks like, we will still be his servants with work to do. The word for work John used here is the same one they would use for the priests' job; we will be *ministering* to God.

Now, don't get any wrong ideas about how boring serving God would get. If you like what you are doing and you regularly have new things to learn and skills to practice, life is amazing and full. I'll tell you what would get torturously boring: amusing yourself for eternity. If you never got to do anything that mattered, just on a kind of lazy vacation forever, you would soon feel so empty and pointless you would want out. God isn't going to punish us like that, he's interesting enough to keep us happy forever.

It is mind-blowing to think of being able to see God and survive. But the idea in **verse 4** is even bigger than that. Have you ever seen someone famous? They are hard to get close to. Since early times it was only special people who were allowed to be near enough to the ruler to see him in person. Joseph used the phrase "see my face" to warn his brothers he would refuse to negotiate with them unless they brought their brother Benjamin (Genesis 43:3). When Pharaoh was seriously ticked at Moses he told him never to "see his face" again (Exodus 10:28).

We will have personal, direct access to the God of the universe. And his name will be part of us. Ask an adult what it's like when you find an important ID paper is missing, or what happens to someone when they have their passport stolen. It's a scary mess. But someday we don't have to worry about ever being locked out or forgotten. God's family ID will be shining on our faces for all to see.

Verse 5 used to make me sad. Not that I like falling asleep, but catching some Z's is kind of fun! Remember, just because the city is never dark doesn't mean there won't be any spot in the universe to go stargazing—you'll just have to get far away from the city glow to do it. And won't it be nice not to have the scary and uncomfortable parts of the night gone forever? God will be there, safer and stronger than the best dad in the world.

Well, that's the end of the prophecy. Everything from this point on is recap and closing statements. John was given enough to make us homesick, but not so much we can't function during the time we are assigned to work here on the current earth.

It's kind of interesting that John doesn't introduce the next person talking to us. It's all been "his" revelation; of course we'll figure out he's still talking. And Jesus wraps things up a lot like he opened it. You can trust what this book tells us. God wants us to know what he's up to, and it's going to happen speedily.

Like the beginning, anyone who holds onto the prophecies we've just read will be blessed.

Verses 8–9 tell us the vision hadn't totally faded as John was listening to Jesus. He can still see the angel who had been assigned to dump one of God's last judgments on the earth (Remember 21:9), and, he's so overwhelmed by everything he's seen, he bowed down to the angel like you would to a ruler or even a god. But the angel doesn't want such treatment. He reminds us that we may be less impressive than a glowing spirit being, but we humans have the same kind of role in life; we all honor God. And a holy angel helps God's people out, just like we do for each other. Those sweet grandmas who call anyone helpful, "angels," aren't so wrong after all! The only one we are to bow low to is God.

The rest of the book seems to be dictated straight from Jesus himself. First, he tells John to leave the prophecy open for anyone to read. It's not like back in Daniel's day (12:9) when the meaning was closed to him and everyone else. Now it's exposed for those able to recognize it. Every Christian from that time on has been expected to live as if Jesus could come in their lifetime.

Verses 11–12 are serious ones. At some point, when we have learned what God says well enough to decide whether we want to obey him or not, he lets us have what we have chosen. We saw this when the Earth Dwellers experienced God's punishment and they still refused to repent or worship him (Revelation 9:20–21). But this verse also reminds us that God will keep those who choose righteousness and holiness from being warped.

There is a reason God warns us that "today" if you will listen, don't harden your hearts (Psalm 95:7–8; Hebrews 4:7). People do get hard and we wouldn't want him to give up on us the way he did those in Noah's day (Genesis 6:3).

Not only is dishonoring God disastrous, serving him is fabulous! Paul tells us in **2 Corinthians 4:17–18** that anything we go through now—even a tortured death and the loss of everything we hold dear—is nothing compared to how amazing Jesus's rewards are. And **Matthew 6:20** tells us these eternal treasures can never, ever be taken away from us.

If we could see how much Jesus is going to reward us for what we do with our lives now, most of us would make wildly different choices on both big and small things.

Remember how Paul told us in **1 Corinthians 3:10–15** the accomplishments of our mortal lives will follow us into eternity—if they don't get burnt to the foundation. Nothing we do can change his love for us, but we get to change a lot of other things about our forever experience. Some people will have spent their time doing things that won't count for anything. Others will have built with the kinds of materials the New Jerusalem is made from.

Jesus tells us in John 15 what it takes to switch from deeds that will burn up to those that matter. If we let him pull us out of the dirt of sin, prune us (John 15:2), and learn to "abide" in his love (verses 4–11) he will help us produce a life he can reward.

It's a win/win for us: he gives us everything we need to do good works and then rewards us because we let him do stuff through us!

Remember how God is the one with the eternal throne in the New Jerusalem? Even though God the Father is the one we focus our worship on, you cannot split him from Jesus. Our Redeemer and Brother is just as much God as the Father is.

Verses 14–15 remind us that the goal we all long for, life and citizenship in the Eternal City, is only for those who do things God's way. It's not saying only people who never do anything bad get in; if it was, God's city would be empty. But we have to submit to God who tells us only Jesus is the way, the truth, and the life.

No one gets close to God without surrendering to him (John 14:6) and his commandment is to *love* God and others (Matthew 22:37–39). All the things in verse 15 describe ways people *use* people and *hate* God. Jesus's people can fall into sin, but they won't be content to live there. David was a "man after God's own heart" but he messed around with his warrior's wife, then had him murdered to cover the crime. God didn't throw David out for this, he rebuked and restored him.

Remember how Jesus was walking in the middle of the seven churches back in chapter one? He still is talking not just to you and me, but to our church families. He wants our local communities to study and understand these things, so we can be there for each other when times get rough.

Take a minute to think about what Jesus is saying when he calls himself both the "root" and the descendant of David. This means David first came from Jesus and then Jesus came through David's family. It is incredible to think of how God first invented people and then became one.

Jesus calls himself after the planet Venus, the Morning Star. This is the 3rd brightest object in our sky. It always glows where the sun is just over the horizon because Venus orbits closer to the sun than we do. Where it shines, the sun isn't far away.

Verse 17 could be our life verse, "Come!" Both the Holy Spirit and all of us already in God's kingdom are calling out to everyone to join us. All of us have been seriously thirsty at some point. The only thing we can think about is water to restore our body. What water is to our thirst, Jesus is to our souls if we are willing. It's free; we just have to ask him.

It is easy to mess up **verses 18–19**. Lots of people "take away" from Jesus's Revelation by ignoring it, but this doesn't mean they won't be allowed into God's city. You have to claim this book isn't God's word to fall under that curse. And there have been people who claim their words are part of the Bible even though this was the last book written. There is no way someone who really belongs to Jesus would pretend to have words so perfect other people should treat them as God's own. These verses are both serious, but shouldn't scare us into not studying what God has told us. Just make sure you don't claim to be inspired by the Holy Spirit to change his Word!

We only have two more verses left in the whole Bible. And how does Jesus spend these last sentences? To remind us the way things are now isn't going to last much longer. He is for-sure coming, and it's going to happen fast.

How do John and everyone who loves Jesus respond? "Amen, just so. Come, Master Jesus!"

Lots of letters in the New Testament end with the closing in **verse 21**. But wishing Jesus's grace on someone is far more than closing with "sincerely yours." If we have Jesus's favor giving us all the good things he wants for us, we have everything anyone could ever want or need. When the time comes for the great transfer of power we will need his help, and we will have it.

I'd love to hear from you how studying these passages has helped you see life differently. I know my own life has been shaped since I was a child by my longing to have as much reward when Jesus calls me home as I can. Who you are, what you care about, and what you do with yourself depends on how you see your life. When you see the future for what God tells us it actually is, you can live for things that don't get broken or go obsolete the way so many people do.

This is all for sure and certain.

Glossary

- **Antichrist, Little Horn, Lawless One, Beast**: the chief human ruler who takes over the world and does his best to destroy Jesus's people while saying terrible things about God.
- **Babylon the Great**: the city of commerce that is so evil God has it destroyed forever
- **Celestial Disturbances**: the darkening of the sun, moon, and stars (along with outer space "rolling up like a scroll") that are signs it's now time for God to avenge his people and reclaim the earth.
- **Dragon, Satan, that Old Serpent, the Devil**: once an angel in charge of worshipping God, now his bitter enemy who wants all the worship for himself and to cause God as much pain as he can while he can.
- **Earth Dwellers**: those who only care about their mortal life and want nothing to do with God's kingdom.
- **Eternal State**: the way heaven and earth will be set up after God the Father causes the current universe to flee to nowhere.
- **False Prophet, Dragon-Lamb**: the human sidekick of the Antichrist focused on inspiring the worship of the Earth Dwellers and punishment of Jesus's people who refuse.
- **The Lamb**: a name for Jesus showing what he has won by sacrificing himself as our human brother.
- **Mystery Babylon**: the false religious system/center that drugs the nations into evil worship. She is destroyed by the Beast's kings.
- **Pivot Point**: a spot in a prophecy where you can tell it's moved from one layer of events to a new timeframe.
- **Tribulation**: Persecution, distress, pressure. How people and spiritual beings treat those whose worldviews they hate.
- **Saints**: Jesus's people, usually humans, sometimes could mean angels too
- **The Woman**: spiritual Israel with all of God's people, including Jesus, as her children

Expand your Study

Even though this book has a lot, it's only covering the framework of a single biblical topic—the future. There is so much more to discover in the Bible and you don't have to wait for someone to study it out for you, there are tools available today that make it possible for everyone to find things for themselves.

There are offline programs you can download onto your computer or device but they tend to only have a few Bible translations to compare and maybe an old commentary or two. I like the Blue Letter Bible app for researching and reading, but it has to be on the internet to help me with the original languages. The other app and website I used a lot to see how different translations interpret concepts is Bible Gateway.

If you have a word or even phrase that gets used repeatedly, you can have your app show you all the places it occurs in English. You can also see what the original language word—usually marked with its "Strong's Concordance Number"—means and find places it was used to get a sense for its "semantic range," which just means how many definitions it has.

Another great way to find more verses on a single idea is to look up cross references. Blue Letter Bible has excellent lists and your print Bible might even have some. There is also a free tool called the *Dictionary of Bible Themes* you can use to study all kinds of topics. This isn't like any dictionary you've used before, instead, it breaks down biblical ideas into categories and links every claim to a passage the authors got it from. Bible Hub has it as well as Bible Gateway (it's just hard to find).

Now What?

Before you do anything else, have you chosen for yourself the only place of eternal protection and truth? The difference between trusting in ourselves and hiding in Jesus can be so subtle many wise people have missed it. But asking Jesus to cleanse and rescue you from sin and eternal death only takes a moment. Everything we have studies shows us how much better it is to belong to God's family than it is to go our own way.

If you have finally understood what it means to belong to God's kingdom through this book, or if you have now decided to take your Christian life seriously, let your family and church know. And I would love to know too. You'll find my contact info at the end of the book and I would be thrilled to talk to you about what you have learned. If you have any questions, I might not have the answers, but I know some wise people who might be able to help you.

Did you like this book? Tell a friend!

Any book you read that isn't on the cover of a Christian catalog needs your help. Every author has to take a lot of time away from their family and writing to tell people about their book. The more help they get from their readers the more writing they can do.

If you enjoyed what I taught here and would like to see other people understand the Bible better, tell them. I have some memes you can share on social media on my website, TheEndStudy.com, to make it easy. Word-of-mouth is the gold standard for any business. Jesus told us to learn from the world how to get his truth out to as many people as we can, without doing anything slimy, in Luke 16:8–11.

And I'm not the only one you can help out this way; every author you read longs for quality reviews online. When you're thinking about spending money on a product you've never used, don't you check the reviews? We all do. You can help me out on whatever platform you got this book from, and while you're there, thank another author too. Once you've logged in, it's easy to show them your appreciation this way.

KEY Ideas

One of the powers of a Bible study is finding the answers for yourself. Scattered throughout this book I've marked the big ideas God hid in his Word to guide our understanding of prophecy, theology, and even our lives. If you write small enough, you can list the references here and I recommend you note them in your Bible as well. Another option is to use the blank space at the end of a book or at the back of your Bible to collect them in one place.

About the Author

My fascination with the book of Revelation started in my teens when my mom had us read a chapter a day out loud month after month (she took Revelation 1:3 seriously!). Over the years I've collected clues and listened to all kinds of teachers wrestle with the Bible's prophetic passages. This book is designed to share with you what I teach my own kids: how to take the Bible for what it is without filtering anything out because of what people have taught us.

Then Daniel blessed the God of heaven. Daniel answered and said,

Blessed be the name of God for ever and ever: for wisdom and might are his: And he changeth the times and the seasons: he removeth kings, and setteth up kings: he giveth wisdom unto the wise, and knowledge to them that know understanding:

He revealeth the deep and secret things: he knoweth what is in the darkness, and the light dwelleth with him. I thank thee, and praise thee, O thou God of my fathers, who hast given me wisdom and might, and hast made known unto me now what we desired of thee: for thou hast now made known unto us the king's matter. Daniel 2:19–23

CPSIA information can be obtained
at www.ICGtesting.com
Printed in the USA
BVHW031702290922
648311BV00011B/492

9 781737 671602